Chelsea

The Challenges of Using Sport ...

Chelsea School Research Centre Edition
Volume 10

John Sugden/James Wallis (Eds.)

Football for Peace?
The Challenges of Using Sport for Co-Existence In Israel

Meyer & Meyer Sport

British Library Cataloguing in Publication Data
A catalogue record for this book is available from the British Library

John Sugden∕James Wallis (Eds.)
Football for Peace – The Challenge of Using Sport for Co-Existence In Israel
Oxford: Meyer & Meyer Sport (UK) Ltd., 2007
ISBN: 978-1-84126-181-2

© 2007 by Meyer & Meyer Sport (UK) Ltd.
Aachen, Adelaide, Auckland, Budapest, Graz, Johannesburg,
New York, Olten (CH), Oxford, Singapore, Toronto
Member of the World
Sports Publishers' Association (WSPA)
www.w-s-p-a.org
Printed and bound by: FINIDR, s. r. o., Český Těšín
ISBN: 978-1-84126-181-2
E-Mail: verlag@m-m-sports.com
www.m-m-sports.com

Contents

Foreword

THE DOWN TO EARTH MIRACLE
2000–2003, AND THEREAFTER

Geoffrey Whitfield

It was Highbury, the home of Arsenal Football Club, and it was April 1st 2004. The Bondholders Suite was being used by some 60 Israeli Jews and Arab Christians, Moslems, members of the Druze community, and members of UK Universities. The date, with its associations, could not take away from the fact that a miracle was being experienced, which had its history of 'stepping stones' from 1993, culminating that day in that particular event. That same week, there had been more shootings, killings and acts of violence between the communities in Israel and Palestine, just as in other parts of the world. But this particular mixed group had spent their final day at Highbury, concluding five days together in a Training Camp Programme which had been largely conducted at the Chelsea School on the Eastbourne campus of the University of Brighton.

In the week before, staff from the Chelsea School had prepared the coaches for an intensive, week-long football/ conflict prevention project in Israel in July, 2004. There, several hundred boys and girls, from families in 16 towns in Northern Israel, would play in mixed teams, Jew with Arab versus Jew with Arab. If a team was to win, Jews and Arab Christians with Arab Moslems would need to learn to trust and have confidence in each other, to work together and thereby gain the victory.

This 'miracle' became possible because of a three year programme which had been created earlier by World Sports Peace Project. It was conceived in 2000, shortly before the outbreak of the Second *Intifada* and continued thereafter, despite warnings of danger, and against a continuous background of charges of 'terrorism' and 'state terrorism'. Despite the issues of security becoming an increasing reality, year after year the conduct of the projects never faltered, but rather continued to expand. Our presence at Highbury that day in April, 2004, was because, from its infancy in 1996 and the early days of planning, Arsenal Football Club had been a significant player in supporting the project.

From 2000 onwards, different communities in Israel were gradually brought together on an annual basis and very quickly the project grew in Ibillin near Nazareth, from 100 youngsters in 2001, to more than 300 from six towns in 2003. Moreover, it drew to itself not only grassroots Arab and Jewish communities in Israel, but the involvement of the British Embassy, the British Council and the Israeli Sports Authority. The participation of staff and student volunteers from the University of Brighton in 2001 was of pivotal importance and grew to include four universities in 2003. A UK coaching team of eight in 2001 became a group of 21 in 2003. And these were still early days.

The relevance of such a project could be clearly seen as Jewish and Arab children learned to feel less fearful of each other and more comfortable in each other's presence. To have in the same team both Arabs and Jews who had to play together and find a spirit of confidence has had significant effects both for the present and the future. It affected not merely the youngsters involved at the time, but the families to whom they returned each day, and their peers, schools and communities.

This was not done in private, but was in the public domain, and towns had different factors to consider at such a time of tension. People who were fearful of each other were being introduced to a new dimension: that people could find ways of being together and so replace their anxiety with confidence and trust. Towns could know ahead of time that their families would be having significant, close interaction of a positive and enjoyable nature which could continue year on year. This contrasted with the atmosphere of suspicion, fear and even hatred that existed in other communities which had not had this kind of opportunity. Those involved would never forget their first-hand experience. Indeed, they would tell their children and grandchildren of that time in their lives, and the consequences for their villages and societies.

So how could the first small project in 2001 change the face of a nation like Israel or any other nation? The answer is that it provided a three-year track record of a viable alternative to terrorism and violence which worked with the grassroots of communities and, with international connections, brought together the younger generation of families and communities. It provided a simple, constructive and pleasurable project so that the participants could experience the strength and common sense of working creatively with a model which they could see would be relevant to their social and political situation. Moreover it came to be recognised as such and was taken up by other organisations thereafter.

The project became a powerful and dynamic alternative to the mistrust, misery, oppression and revenge in many parts of the land, when emotions were fanned by a cycle of vicious retaliation and blame. Such experiences affected the fabric of each community which became threatened with fear and animosity. Each community had its history of horror stories, but had not yet become strong enough to move ahead to find solutions that would be viable for their children and grandchildren. This scheme had begun as a dream and vision in 2000 until its completion as a three-year experiment in 2003. In the future, its track record of success and learning curves will be taken on by those with the resources to develop it on a national and international scale. The second three-year period has already seen similar projects springing up throughout Israel. After 2003, the combined resources of the University of Brighton, the British Council and the Israel Sports Authority extended the project in Israel and made it commonplace in the wider territory. Hopefully this will also be developed even further in the future with the appropriate authorities in Palestine.

While for many involved the project was a purely secular affair, for some, including this author, the philosophy behind the project had a theological base, but one which did not need to be specifically expressed or emphasised because, invisibly, it was enshrined in the project's origins. The tradition of Christian humanitarian involvement goes back through the centuries, and one can easily look back to the English thinkers and reformers of the nineteenth century and pick out William Wilberforce, Charles Kingsley, Charles Dickens and many others. They combined with people of a range of different persuasions in order to achieve the success of their projects. This twenty-first century project was part of that tradition of innovative involvement in the principles and practice of conflict prevention and resolution in humanitarian terms, in which unspoken theological or political perspectives did not need to be spelt out. What created the teamwork was the unspoken agenda that the project was the right thing to do: that was the principle that the participants had in common, rather than holding to any narrow formula.

The ongoing excellence of the volunteer staff and coaches from the Chelsea School brought initiatives which led to the involvement of other UK universities on an annual basis, and has been essential in building permanent alliances with coaches from the local communities. Together, these could create a structure whereby the programme becomes more than an annual event, but one that is established on a regular basis in the Arab and Jewish communities. This kind of project is for export, and can be translated into other sports and activities on a large scale. That is conflict prevention; that is peace-making on the ground, and that brings hope for a different future on a global scale. As a mark of this, a letter was received just before the third project in 2003 from someone who knew all about conflict and reconciliation and had been supportive as the project developed. He wrote:

> Dear Geoffrey
> Congratulations on the fruits of what can only be an immense amount of hard work and commitment from yourself and many others. It is indeed 'marvellous in our eyes'. God is good.
> My warm greetings to all concerned. This is wonderful.
> God bless you.
> Archbishop Desmond Tutu

In September 2003, I (Geoffrey Whitfield) and David Bedford, the co-founders, entrusted the project we had commenced in 2000 to The Chelsea School at the University of Brighton and the British Council in Israel. It is now known as Football for Peace (F4P)[1]. Since then it has grown beyond all expectation. As the British Ambassador to Israel, His Excellency, Sherard Cowper-Coles, said at the tournament prize- giving in the summer of 2004, "from small acorns such as these, giant trees will grow". We anticipate the growth of the forest!

Note

[1]   Today F4P is a secular organisation that is underpinned by a principle of neutrality and is not affiliated with any religious or political groups.

ABOUT THE AUTHORS

Michael Boyd is Community Relations Officer for the IFA (Irish Football Association). He studied at the University of Ulster, Jordanstown and has a BA (Hons) in Sport Studies and MSc in Communications, Public Relations and Advertising. As a youngster Michael represented Northern Ireland at Under Fifteen level. In 2000 he became one of the youngest ever European A Licensed football coaches in Northern Ireland. He has also coached in the US and China. Michael is heavily involved in coaching disability football in Northern Ireland and acts as a Tutor on the IFA's Coaching Disabled Footballers Award and B Licence Coach Education Programmes.

Dr. Jayne Caudwell is senior lecturer in the sociology of sport and leisure cultures at the Chelsea School, University of Brighton. Her teaching and research includes a focus on gender, sexuality and women's experiences of football cultures. She plays and coaches football.

John Doyle is a Research Assistant in the University of Brighton's Chelsea School. As part of his job, John oversees the evaluation of the Football for Peace Project. Based on the development of innovative visual recording techniques, he is currently working on his PhD which focuses on the efficacy of sport-based community relations interventions in divided societies.

Chris Howarth studied Sport and Exercise Science at the University of Brighton, Chelsea School between 2002 and 2005. He has been involved in F4P since 2002 and has progressed to become one of the projects' most experienced coaches and became a project leader in 2005. Currently, Chris is a Research assistant in Sport and Exercise Science at the University of Brighton.

John Lambert is a Senior Lecturer in Physical Education at the University of Brighton. He specializes in research and consultancy in Physical Education and Sport. He is a UEFA A License Coach and works within the talent identification programme at a Barclays Premiership football club in England.

Ghazi Nujidat is a Regional Director (Galilee) of the Israeli Sports Authority and official coordinator for Football for Peace. Along with the British Council, Ghazi oversees the selection of the participant Jewish and Arab communities and, facilitates communications between them in the build up to and during the Project.

Gary Stidder is a former secondary school teacher and is currently a Senior Lecturer in Physical Education at the University of Brighton. He is co-editor (with Sid Hayes) of *Equity and Inclusion in PE and Sport* published by Routledge (2003), holds the University award for teaching excellence, and is a founder member of the Football for Peace Project in Israel.

John Sugden is Professor in the Sociology of Sport at the University of Brighton. He has researched and written extensively about sport in divided societies and is a co-founder of Football for Peace. Professor Sugden is the Editor of the *International Review for the Sociology of Sport*.

Stuart Townsend studied for 2 years on a soccer scholarship at Colorado Christian University, Denver, USA before entering the University of Brighton's Physical Education programme and graduating from there in 2004. Currently, Stuart is Deputy Head of the Department of Physical Education at Dorothy Stringer High School, Brighton, a comprehensive 11–16 school with specialist sport college status. Stuart volunteered as a project coach in 2004 and returned in 2005 with support from his school to identify the potential for an increased values based emphasis in an English PE curriculum.

James Wallis is a Senior Lecturer in Physical Education at the Chelsea School, University of Brighton. He taught in Secondary and Further Education sectors before completing a Masters degree in Sport and Exercise Science and joining Chelsea School in 2001. He has worked on F4P for three years as a project leader.

Geoffrey Whitfield is a retired Baptist Minister, psychotherapist and former University Chaplain. He has worked and written about the Israel-Palestine situation for ten years and is currently researching into the causes of terrorism with the Human Rights and Social Justice Research Institute of London Metropolitan University.

Chapter 1

INTRODUCTION:
FOOTBALL FOR PEACE IN CONTEXT

John Sugden

Football for Peace (F4P) is a joint University of Brighton and British Council initiative that aims to use values-based football coaching to build bridges between neighbouring Jewish and Arab towns and villages in Israel, and in doing so make a modest contribution to the peace process in this troubled region. The work of F4P seeks to make pragmatic and incremental grass-roots interventions into the sport culture of Israel, helping to build bridges between otherwise divided communities and at the same time make a contribution to political/policy debates around sport in the region. Specifically its fourfold aims are to: provide opportunities for social contact across community boundaries; promote mutual understanding; engender in participants a desire for and commitment to peaceful coexistence; and enhance soccer skills and technical knowledge. This chapter overviews the history and development of the project before focusing on the 2005 initiative.

Social and political context

Those wishing to use sport to promote social reform need first to carefully dissect the nature of the sport experience in both its natural setting and broader social and historical context. The conflict in Israel and Palestine has deep historical roots and widespread and complex contemporary manifestations. For the purpose of this introduction, only a brief outline of the key socio-political and demographic features that are the most pertinent to F4P can be outlined. The state of Israel was controversially created in 1948

1

in the long shadow of World War II. While this can be seen as a major achievement for the hitherto nation-less and persecuted Jewish people, in equal measure it can be viewed as a disaster for the Palestinians on whose land the fledging state took shape (Said, 2000). In 1948 only 160,000 Arabs stayed in Israel; the rest, some 640,000, fled — mainly to neighbouring Jordan, Syria and Lebanon (today the Palestinian diaspora number is in the region of 3.5 million). Approximately 2.5 million Palestinians live in the Occupied Territories (West Bank and Gaza), some of the most densely populated places on earth. Perhaps rightly so, the situation of the Palestinians within the Occupied Territories, the plight of the Palestinian Diaspora, and the Israeli State's engagement with these external factors attract most global attention. However, often forgotten by the international community, and the main concern of this paper, is the status of relations between the Jews and the Arabs who remained within the state of Israel after 1948.

The late and highly respected Palestinian academic and activist Edward Said believed that co-existence, not separation, is the way forward if a lasting peace is to be achieved in Israel. He points out, "we cannot coexist as two communities of detached and uncommunicatingly separate suffering ... the only way of rising beyond the endless back-and-forth violence and dehuman-isation is to admit the universality and integrity of the other's experience and to begin to plan a common life together" (Said, 2002: p. 208). Likewise, Naim Ateek, a senior Christian-Arab cleric, argues that any lasting peace in the region must be based upon reconciliation which itself is dependent upon mutual recognition of and respect for different cultural traditions and the history of oppression and suffering that underpins those traditions: "Before the process of peacemaking can begin, a change in attitude of Israeli Jews and Palestinians towards one another is necessary. They need to face each other with candour, to create the new attitudes that will be the foundation for peace and stability in the region" (Ateek, 1989: p. 168).

By the year 2000, Jewish Israelis numbered approximately 5.5 million, made up of a mixture of migrant first generation European and Americans, Ethiopian Jews (Falash Mura), and more recent arrivals from the former Soviet Union. While in terms of religious persuasion the majority of the Jewish population consider themselves to be secular, a significant minority are devoted adherents to the Hebrew faith. This religious orthodoxy is a key dimension of Israel's fractured political make-up. The number of 'Palestinian-Arab-Israeli' citizens is approximately 1.2 million, roughly 18 percent of the population. This too is an exceedingly complex identity. The order of its wording changes depending upon the political consciousness of the individual bearing it. It is further complicated via the religious and ethnic suffixes that can be added: Moslem (Sunni and Shiite); Christian; Druze; and so forth, not to mention more tribal affiliations such as the Bedouin and Circassians (nineteen century migrants from Eastern Europe's North Caucuses), which also inform the mapping of the county's sectarian geography.

F4P is based in Galilee in the north east of the country, a region with towns and villages with names such as Nazareth, Cana, Tiberias and Megiddo, evocative of the region's biblical past. Modern Galilee's population (1.146 million) makes up 17 percent of the overall population. Two-thirds of the Galilee's residents are at the bottom of the socioeconomic scale. About half of them — 46 percent — are Arabs, mostly Moslem, but with a large minority of Christians. The unemployment rate in the Galilee is some 50 percent higher than the national one. In the more rural areas of Galilee, Jews and Arabs live in separate towns and villages, whereas in the larger urban areas, such as Akko and neighbouring Haifa, the two communities live in separate enclaves. Travelling between them, it is clear to the observer that the Jewish communities are considerably better off than their Arab counterparts who feature disproportionately in ranks of the region's socio-economically deprived. Official statistics confirm this is the case (Sa'ar, 2004).

Sport and football in Israeli society

Outside of the Middle East, good examples of how sport can contribute to peace processes can be found in South Africa and Northern Ireland. In the former case, sport was one of the most important fronts in the struggle against apartheid. In the post-apartheid era, sport has a new role as a medium through which the diverse and formerly antagonistic elements of the 'rainbow nation' are reconciled and harmonised (Keim, 2003). In Northern Ireland, where sport was once a theatre for the expression of cross-community animosity, sport is now formally recognised as a key element in the peace process. However, as research carried out in Northern Ireland tells us, the view that any sport and all sport is a universal social good is extremely naïve (Sugden, 2004; Bairner, 2001).

Like everything else in Israel, sport is highly politicised. It is an important sphere of civil society and is terrain contested between Jews and Arabs and the various factions within each community. The politically contested dimension of Israeli sport has increased in proportion to the increasing numbers of Israeli-Arabs who choose to participate (Sorek, 2003). Until relatively recently, other than at the margins in sectarian places and spaces, football for Arabs in Israel was another contested aspect of mainstream civil society wherein they were losing out. Traditionally, professional football in Israel has been linked to mainly Jewish political parties and political associations, including trades unions. In addition, as Ben-Porat (2000) has argued, along with other state-sponsored sports and sporting organisations, after 1948 football was an integral part of the process through which the cultural façade of the (Jewish) state of Israel was constructed. This made it difficult for Israeli Arabs to participate at the highest levels. It also helped to exacerbate problems for Israel's participation in international football competitions, leading the world governing body Fifa to the radical step of taking Israel out of the AFC (Asian Football Confederation) to avoid confrontation with regional Arab states, and placing them first within the OFC (Oceania–Australasia and the South Pacific), and latterly within Uefa (Europe) for future World Cup qualification purposes (Sugden and Tomlinson, 1998: p. 239). As we shall see, the decision made by Fifa in 1998 to readmit Palestine into the 'Fifa family' — even though Palestine is not recognised internationally as a nation-state — has led to problems for some talented Israeli Arab Palestinians who now have to decide to which football 'nation' should they owe allegiance (Taylor, 2004).

However, in the wake of post 1967 modernisation of Israeli society and the advance of post 1980s globalisation, things began to change with evidence of a professional/commercial, performance pragmatic at work through which professional football became more open to the participation of Arab players and Arab-owned teams: "The globalisation and liberalisation of Israeli society since the 1980s and the waning power of the political parties (the former patrons of soccer) have facilitated the commercialization of the game, introducing a profit motive and economic rationality of both players and owners" (Ben-Porat and Ben-Porat, 2004: p. 433). In other words, it is good business to recruit the best players, regardless of their race or ethnic/national identity because this produces better teams and more success. The net result of this is that, perhaps impelled by relative impoverishment and the perceived riches available in professional sport, more and more Arabs are taking up opportunities to play and watch football in settings that were formerly the almost exclusive preserve of the Jews. This tendency has been encouraged by breakthroughs made by both Jewish and

Arab players from Israel who play in the most prestigious professional European leagues. It is for these reasons that Sorak (2002) has been able to argue that football, more than any other sporting sphere, has the potential to be an 'integrative enclave' in Israel.

This advance does not come without the creation of other problems. Precisely because more Arab players, teams, and their fans are now taking part, football also offers more opportunities for racial and ethno-national confrontation. For instance, 'death to the Arabs' and other, unprintable and more profane, racially vicious chants are sometimes heard coming from the exclusively Jewish terraces of Beitar Jerusalem, the team which is consistently at the top of the NIF's (New Israel Fund) weekly racism incitement index. This initiative was introduced in 2004 into the Israeli football league in recognition of the increase in sectarian-related incidents in and around the country's football stadiums. As well as working with the NIF, the IFA (Israeli Football association) is also consulting with representatives from The FA (the English Football Association), who with their long experience of dealing with racism in English football are helping them to devise anti-racist strategies which are most suitable for the local context (FA, 2005).

Linked to the theme of equity and inclusion, and given that one of F4P's objectives is to get more girls and women involved, another important contextual issue is concerned with the relatively underdeveloped state of women's sport in Israel. As one report puts it:

> In general terms it might be said that women have never had the encouragement to take up competitive sport in the same way that men have. Research has shown that in Israel only about 25% of the participants in competitive sport are women, a number much lower than the average in the western world, and even lower than the average in the word as a whole. (Israel, 2004: p. 2)

This view is confirmed by the results of a survey carried out in 2000 by the Israel Women's Network which revealed that of all registered athletes in 15 major sports only 24% were female. Worse was the gender imbalance in football where of a total of 32,000 registered players only 1,000 were female, barely more than 3%. In terms of who runs sport in Israel the situation is equally unbalanced as women are virtually invisible with less than 10% representation. Once more the worst culprit is football. Even though Israel inaugurated a women's league in 1998, the Israeli Football Association (IFA) has no female representatives on the governing body (Israel Women's Network, 2002).

In 1995 the Ministry of Education in Israel adopted the 'Brighton Declaration on Women and Sport' requiring government and volunteer organisations to promote gender equality in sport and to establish special programmes to ensure due representation of women at all levels and in all entities (Israel Women's Network, 2002). It would appear that there is still a long way to go. As will be illustrated later in the book, however, in addition to pointing to male privilege, any explanation for the under-representation of women in sport in Israel must take account of a complex range of local factors, not the least of which are religious in nature.

Project history and development[1]

The first formal phase of the F4P project began modestly in 2001 when six volunteer coaches from the University of Brighton and one staff leader conducted a week-long coaching camp in the Arab town of I'blin. The timing could hardly have been worse as operations began during the height of the second *Intafada* (uprising). The key difference between this and other popular anti-Israeli protests was that it spilled out of the Palestinian Authority and drew in Palestinian Arabs living as citizens within the state of Israel. They took to the streets to protest against the brutal means being used by the Israeli authorities to quell the unrest in the Palestinian Authority as well as to draw attention to their perceived lack of civil rights within Israel itself. In response to such protests, in Israeli-Arab towns such as Nazareth and Sakhnin (both now partners in the F4P project), the security forces reacted very aggressively as a result of which many Arab-Israeli citizens were arrested and some were killed or seriously injured (Said, 2002). This grievously damaged already fragile cross-community relations between Arabs and Jews within Israel in general, and in the region of Galilee in particular. The increasing use of suicide bombers as a strategy for resistance by a variety of Palestinian extremist groups exacerbated a growing cross-community mistrust and polarization.

For the 2001 football project, the original plan had been to partner I'blin with a nearby Jewish municipality, but with lines of communication all but down, and in the wake of a bus bombing in the neighbourhood, the ensuing security situation caused the Jewish community to withdraw their children from the project at the eleventh hour. The 2001 project went ahead nonetheless in I'blin, involving 100 Muslim Arab and Christian Arab children (10–

14 years old). This reflected the sectarian geography of the town of I'blin where Moslems and Christians lived in separate neighbourhoods. As we have seen, community divisions in the region are more complex than simply between monolithic blocs of Arabs and Jews: rifts and tensions within the Arab community in Galilee was a dimension of the problem that the UK team had not previously appreciated or accounted for. This in itself was an important learning experience. In the face of all the odds, and despite the absence of a Jewish partner, the fact that the project took place at all was a considerable achievement, demonstrating that from a logistical point of view — fund raising, volunteer recruitment, planning, travel, provision of equipment, program execution, and so forth — such programmes could be successfully mounted.

Building upon this qualified success, the following year a second project took place involving a slightly expanded team of eight coaches and two staff leaders. This time, in addition to I'blin the co-operation of the Jewish communities of Misgav and Tivon was secured allowing 150 Arab and Jewish children, including 20 girls, to share the coaching and playing experience. The inclusion of girls training separately but alongside the boys was not universally approved and this issue was to emerge later as one of our biggest challenges.

Local volunteer coaches and community sport leaders were more involved in the planning of the 2002 event and participated fully in the coaching project. The involvement of local people and their increasing sense of partnership/ownership was perceived as a very important development and a key area in terms of the project's longer term sustainability.

In 2003 F4P once more doubled in size, involving twelve UK coaches and three leaders running three simultaneous projects, in six different locations, working with 300 children and 30 volunteer coaches from six communities widespread throughout Galilee. The 2003 event also involved for the first time a pre-project training day during which, once they had arrived in Israel, the UK volunteers and leaders worked alongside their Arab and Jewish colleagues in preparation for the forthcoming week's programme. Once the project-proper started, parallel with the football coaching, there was a programme of 'off-pitch' activities whereby those age groups of children who were not involved with the football engaged with a variety of community relations activities designed and led by local leaders and volunteers. Some of these were recreationally based while others required more of an intellectual input.

By this time the British Council in Israel had grown to become a key partner with the University of Brighton in the development, management, fund raising and administration of F4P. The British Council is a well-established global organisation with a proven commitment to social and cultural development and education. The special circumstances of Israel's conflict-ridden society meant that the British Council there had added community relations work to its portfolio of activities. In F4P they saw an opportunity to promote this dimension of their mission through sport while at the same time drawing on the expertise and excellence of volunteers trained in UK universities. In return, from its main offices in Tel Aviv and East Jerusalem and its sub office in Nazareth, the British council were able to furnish F4P with a local administrative hub from which year-round planning and networking could take place with communities taking part in the project. The British Council were also key in getting the Israeli Sports Authority (ISA) involved in the project. As is explained in greater detail in Chapter 10, the ISA soon became the most important factor in developing and communicating with the growing network of participating communities and it is largely through them that the longer term sustainability of F4P has been so much enhanced.

All who had been key participants agreed that the 2003 project was a great success. However, during the post-project evaluations, and in anticipation of facilitating a further project in 2004, some significant issues emerged. Firstly, it was determined that, even though the football coaching had been much appreciated by the children, we had to ensure that what we were achieving was more than simply improvements in football skills. The team felt that they needed to do more to ensure that the contents of that football programme were clearly underpinned by values and principles that fed a broader community relations agenda, and that those values and principles were appreciated by the local coaches and experienced by the children in practice.

Related to this, it became clear that the 'off-pitch' activities had not been universally successful. Getting youngsters to play together is one thing, but placing them in situations where they had to talk about and confront some of the more sensitive features of their divided society is far more problematic. Engagement with this kind of work requires levels of training and expertise that neither the UK team nor most of the local facilitators possessed. The F4P team concluded that at this stage this kind of intervention was beyond the remit of the project. If not done well, there was a danger that bad feelings engendered in some of the 'off-pitch' activities would undermine the positive work taking place within the football programme.

Rather than ignore this issue we determined to rethink the ways in which we used the on-pitch activities and we set out to design a soccer coaching manual that would provide opportunities for social contact across community boundaries, promoted mutual understanding, and engendered in participants — children and coaches alike — a desire for and commitment to peaceful coexistence. In addition, of course, we aimed to enhance soccer skills and technical knowledge, but this was very much secondary to the broader community relations aims. The resulting coaching manual emphasises neutrality, equity and inclusion, respect, trust, and responsibility and contains a series of football practices and exercises through which children's learning and understanding of these principles and values can be made manifest. A pilot version of the F4P Coaching Manual was produced in March 2004 (Lambert, Stidder and Sugden, 2004) and was used in the next phase of the project in Israel in July later that year. Chapter 2 provides full details of the development of this Manual.

The 2004 main event was more than twice the size of previous F4P programmes. It involved 700 children from 16 communities throughout Northern Israel. In its execution, a team of 28 student-volunteer coaches and seven leaders from the UK worked alongside 60 local, Jewish and Arab-Israeli volunteers at seven different project sites, including a girls-only project in Tiberias on the banks of the Sea of Galilee.

The initiation of a girls-only project staffed entirely by female coaches and translators was in response to our own evaluations and feedback from local sources who favoured the inclusion of girls but were also sensitive to regional and religious customs and traditions with regard to gender issues. As will be made abundantly clear in some of the following chapters (especially Chapter 7), it can be problematic taking values germane to Western societies and attempting to articulate them through sport in Oriental and other non-western cultures. Even if desirable, crude attempts to impose self-defined 'universal' values are unlikely to work. The desire to achieve equity and inclusion, while at the same time being respectful of local customs and religious traditions, can raise tensions and problems which can only be resolved through adopting a pragmatic approach. The introduction of the girls-only project should be viewed in this light.

The 2005 F4P programme was the largest and most ambitious since its inception in 1999–2000. Broadly, it followed the pattern of the 2004 project, with a training week for Jewish and Arab coaches from Israel and UK volunteers held at the University of Brighton during March 2005, followed in July by the main project in Israel. This consisted of a parallel series of eight, 5-day long coaching projects involving 18 different communities and approximately 1,000 Jewish and Arab children. The July project followed what was becoming a familiar pattern beginning with a training day for local coaches, followed by four days of coaching with the F4P Manual. On day one of each project the children from the separate communities were placed in mixed coaching groups (n=12). They were mixed according to community identity and football ability ensuring that not only did Arab and Jewish children play alongside one another, but also that when it came to competition time, teams would be evenly matched. As had happened in each of the preceding years, the 2005 enterprise came to a close with a grand finals day and awards ceremony (involving all participants), followed the next day by feedback evaluation morning for all coaches and all community representatives.

Football for Peace — the volume

The rest of this book is dedicated to a detailed account and evaluation of the 2005 adventure. It is written completely by people who worked on the 2005 event, some of whom were first timers while others had volunteered several times before. It is mainly structured around the experiences of team leaders at different project venues involving different cross-community partnerships. The authors were not given a detailed brief other than being told to record accurately and honestly what they believed to be the salient features of their experience and to reflect critically upon them. Where possible they were asked to draw upon the views and experiences of the volunteer coaches in their project teams and to reflect on their experiences of previous year's projects. They were asked to be as objective as possible, and the fact that this was book not a public relations exercise for the University of Brighton, the British Council and the Israeli Sports Authority was emphasised.

The one thing that all the authors have in common is their engagement with F4P. Otherwise they are quite different people with different capacities, experiences and points of view. When they wrote their pieces some were still students and others were Physical Education teachers. A few are University Lecturers, but not all are experienced researchers and writers. Some know little detail of the complex nature of the internecine political conflict that frames all aspects of Israeli society, including F4P. Others are more aware and this informs their view of what a project like F4P can and cannot achieve. Some of the pieces are narrative descriptions while others have a more reflectively critical and theoretical undertone. Each contribution contains its own history and analysis as viewed through the distinctive gaze of each author. As such, what follows is not a company mantra, but an eclectic, reflective and impressionistic portrait of a year in the life of Football for Peace.

Football for Peace is underpinned by a distinctive and values-based coaching curriculum and in Chapter Two the main architect of this curriculum, John Lambert, details the background to its development and outlines its key features. In Chapter Three, James Wallis, recounts the extraordinary experience of working within the very distinctive communities of Megiddo and Um al Fahem and in Chapter Four, John Lambert reflects on his contrasting experiences of running projects in Kfar Kara and Menashe as compared to projects in the Crusader port of Akko.

Based in Belfast, Michael Boyd works as a Community Relations Officer for the Irish Football Association. In Chapter Five he provides observations on his experience of a leading a project in Nazareth and Nahalal and reflects on this in the light of his experiences of living and working in Northern Ireland. Chapter Six, which features a project between Emek Ha Yardain and El Battouf, is written by Gary Stidder but draws heavily on the observations and reflections of Adrian Haasner, a volunteer from the German Sports University in Cologne. In Chapter Seven, Jayne Caudwell, who led a project in I'blin and Misgav, introduces a feminist perspective and in doing so raises some key and controversial issues surrounding the position of women in sport in patriarchal and religiously conservative cultures.

Chris Howarth and Stewart Townsend are two student volunteers who worked as coaches in 2004 and were asked to be project leaders in 2005. In chapters Eight and Nine, they tell their stories and in doing so illustrate how much the experience of working on Football for Peace has influenced their own personal and professional development. Ghazi Nujidat is a Regional Director of the Israeli sports Authority with a particular responsibility for Galilee. Ghazi is a Bedouin Arab and as such is uniquely placed to reflect on the contribution that F4P has made in helping to harmonise relations between Jewish and Arab communities in the area under his jurisdiction. Chapter Ten traces his increasing involvement in and commitment to Football for Peace and gives the book a local perspective.

In the final Chapter, John Doyle, the Project Research Officer, outlines the various ways through which the project has been monitored and evaluated and subjects these processes themselves to critical appraisal.

The book concludes with a postscript which relates what happened to the 2006 project when war broke out along the Israel-Lebanon border in July 2006, and considers the implications of this for the future development of Football for Peace.

Note

1   Those interested in more detail about the project's early beginnings should consult Geoffrey Whitfield's *Amity in the Middle East* (2006), Alpha Press.

References

Ateek, N.(1989) *Justice and only justice*. Maryknoll, NY: Orbis.

Ben-Porat, A. (1998) 'The commodification of football in Israel', *International Review for the Sociology of Sport* Vol. 3, No. 33: pp. 267–267.

Ben-Porat, G and Ben-Porat, A. (2004) '(Un)bounded soccer: Globalization and localization of the game in Israel', *International Review for the Sociology of Sport* Vol. 39, No. 4: pp. 421–436.

FA (2005) 'United they stand on both sides of the line', *Communiqué*, Issue 12.

Israel, S. (2000) 'The story of Sport in Israel', *The Jewish Agency for Israel*, www.jafi.org.il/education, Israel Women's Network (2002).

Keim, M (2003) *Nation building at play: Sport as a tool for integration in post-apartheid South Africa*. Aachen, Meyer and Meyer.

Lambert, J, Stidder, G. and Sugden, J. (2004) *Football for Peace coaching manual*. University of Brighton, Unpublished.

Sa'ar, R (2004) 'Government's financial neglect may cause collapse of Galilee communities', 22 August, 2004, www.haaretz.com.

Said, E. (2002) *The end of the peace process*. London: Granta.

Sorek, T. (2003) 'Arab football in Israel as an "integrative enclave"', in *Ethnic and Racial Studies* Vol. 26, No. 3 (May): pp. 422–450.

Sugden, J. (2004) 'Sport and community relations in Northern Ireland and Israel', in A. Bairner (ed) *Sport and the Irish*. Dublin: University of Dublin Press, pp. 238–251.

Taylor, E. (2004) 'For occupied Palestine, just turning up is a struggle', *The Guardian*, 8 September, 2004: p. 33.

Chapter 2

A VALUES-BASED APPROACH TO COACHING SPORT IN DIVIDED SOCIETIES. THE FOOTBALL FOR PEACE COACHING MANUAL

John Lambert

Introduction

Sport is value neutral insofar as it possesses no intrinsic set of meanings above and beyond its rules, regulations and technical argot. It is people that give sport its ideological content. Depending what values it is laden with, sport can either foster harmonious relations between peoples or generate conflict. Thus, in deeply divided societies, simply getting rival communities to play more sport together does not guarantee that conflict resolution and co-existence will follow. To achieve the latter, the meanings attached to sport and the teaching and learning styles used need to be appropriate to peace-related objectives. Football for Peace (F4P) is a sport-based co-existence project for Jewish and Arab children in Northern Israel. One of its distinguishing features has been the development of a specialist football (soccer) coaching manual. Through a carefully designed series of practical coaching activities, this manual emphasises, animates and embodies a series of values that promote fair play, co-operation , mutual understanding, and aid the cause of conflict prevention and co-existence. This chapter outlines the development of this specialist manual, identifies its key features and, drawing upon empirical data gathered in the UK and Israel over the period 2004–6, critically evaluates its efficacy.

A rationale for the development of the Football 4 Peace Coaching Manual

Whilst getting children to enjoy learning and playing football together in non-threatening settings is one of the guiding principles of F4P, the UK team have learned through experience that, in and of itself, simply playing football is not sufficient to promote the kind of interaction that can allow longer-term relationships and cross-community understanding to flourish. A major innovation for the 2004 initiative, therefore, was the development of the F4P Coaching Manual — the idea behind which is to underpin a technical football coaching programme with values and principles which in practice help to promote mutual understanding and responsible citizenship. Each coaching session has been very carefully designed so that each of F4P's five principles of fair play (neutrality; equity and inclusion; respect; trust; and responsibility) are exemplified through the nature of the football practices being undertaken.

Prior to the 2004 F4P project, the football activities were supported by an off-pitch programme based around personal and social development. The activities took place either immediately prior to or after the football coaching. Trust games, team-building exercises and problem-solving activities were used by local youth leaders and teachers to support the aims of co-existence and peaceful reconciliation. The facilitators of this programme were well-prepared and briefed. Nevertheless the off-pitch social education programme used in Galilee 2003 was not a resounding success. Evaluation of these activities by all interested parties pointed to problems that often led to social division instead of cohesion. The children were not particularly receptive to the group activities due to language barriers, disruptive behaviour and a lack of understanding about why they were doing them in the first place. The group activities were often seen by the children as a less exciting alternative to football. Some observers felt that the fact that the UK coaches were not directly involved in the delivery of the initiative contributed to these problems. The teaching of personal and social education through classroom-based sessions requires specialist approaches which, in turn, necessitates extra training of the teachers involved. Many of the facilitators instead turned out to be enthusiastic and willing volunteers without the necessary personal and social education facilitating skills.

Marion Keim's (2003) *Nation Building at Play* is a study of the effectiveness of sport as a tool for social integration in South Africa. She concludes that quantitative evidence points to sport having a very limited role in 'nation-building' in that country, although in a "qualitative sense the projects produced valuable indicators and insights for a user-centred and practice-oriented approach to sport-related projects for the promotion of social integration between members of different population groups" (p. 177). Interestingly, her research related to experiences that were prevalent with F4P: she found more success with activities that were not explicitly about 'team-building' or social bonding, but that thrust people together in a natural way as part of their structure. Keim, in her work on post-apartheid South Africa, found that social integration was more successful through the medium of sport participation than in a classroom. Her research supports the view that co-existence and conflict prevention is best taught in a more indirect, subliminal way.

The F4P project team responded to the problem of the off-pitch activities by suggesting that the whole programme be based on practical football and general team games activities that put a strong emphasis on social educa-tion. Just 'throwing a ball out' was never going to be enough. In such cir-cumstances football can lead to confrontation and conflict as readily as it can lead to friendship and co-operation . There was discussion as to whe-ther this idea was viable. The consensus of the F4P organising group was that it was, but that a carefully thought-through curriculum would have to be developed in which the values associated with mutual understanding and co-existence would be articulated. The F4P coaching manual was developed and piloted in response to a need for the whole project to be based around football-related themes and activities.

The Jewish and Arab Israeli partners saw the need to retain an off-pitch programme, mainly for logistical reasons. The children were coached in two age groups that usually travelled together in one bus to the venues. Doubling these trips would simply be too expensive, so when one age group were taking part in the football session the other age group needed to be given something constructive to do. These sessions ran parallel to the foot-ball events and consisted mainly of practical activities such as swimming, orienteering and minor games. The only major problem that arose from this programme was when one of the local youth workers led a discussion on the meaning of the Israeli National anthem with the children. This led to one of the girls, who saw herself as very much a Palestinian, leaving the project. Whilst that discussion session, in the opinion of the facilitator, seemed an appropriate activity at the time, in retrospect it did not fit comfortably with the rest of theF4P programme. Whilst this type of discussion has its place in Israeli society, F4P is a politics-free zone and the political discourse that surrounds the conflict has no place in the children's F4P activities[1].

An additional motivation for producing the F4P coaching manual was that the team felt that they needed to do more to ensure that the contents of that football programme were clearly underpinned by values and principles that fed a broader community relations agenda, and that those values and principles were understood and accepted by the local coaches and experienced by the children in practice. There was a also need for a coherent and relevant set of values that could be accepted by all partners across the project. How these values and principles were chosen, adopted and embraced will be related later in this chapter.

Football is certainly not the only sporting, artistic or cultural medium through which peaceful co-existence is being actively encouraged in the Middle East. There are several projects based around music, drama, dance and other sports in the region that bring Muslims, Jews and Christians together in very effective ways. One notable example is Daniel Barenboim's work with the West-Eastern Divan Orchestra. A recent addition to the list is the Encompass Trust Tall Ships project which was initiated in England after the 2002 bombings in Bali. These schemes are admirable in both their aims and deeds in that they involve young people from a variety of communities in activities that promote co-existence in the Middle East.

There are a number of reasons why football is believed to be a suitable and effective activity for the development of personal, social and moral values. One such reason is that it is a universally popular game. 'The people's game', as it has been branded, is the most popular game in the world across nationality, gender, social and class boundaries. The University of Brighton has strong tradition of training PE teachers (20% of the UK total), many of whom have an interest in playing and coaching football. Also, games are not only relatively easy to organise and facilitate but most children love playing football. This is a crucial point to make, in that the young people involved in F4P are first and foremost there to play football. By the end of the week of the 2004 F4P project an association between football, fun and co-existence had gradually developed. The children changed from showing uncertainty about visiting an unfamiliar community to elation as the bus arrived at the pitch and were are back to play with their F4P team. As one of the UK coaches wrote in her evaluation, "It was amazing. The group arrived as two and left as one" (Menashe/Kfar Qara, 2004).

Sorek (2003) has discussed the complex situation in Israel in terms of divisions within sport along religious and ethnic lines and has described Arab football in Israel as an "integrative enclave" (p. 422). He points out that within football there is a great deal of integration and co-existence between Arabs and the Jews. This is not recognised by the Arab press who emphasise the distinctive national identity of the Arab teams and players. The Hebrew media, however, tend to use Arab success in football as evidence for the possible shared citizenship for Arabs and Jews. The emergence of Sakhnin in the professional game in Israel is an intriguing case study of how a mixed religion and racial team can be used by political groups to support their particular viewpoint.

The truth, of course, is that football is all too often a sport that exhibits division, conflict and aggression. Evidence appears in the media every day of instances of players at the elite level behaving in a manner that is contradictory to most, if not all, of the F4P values. It is precisely because of this potential for conflict that it is an appropriate and effective vehicle for this type of co-existence and conflict prevention project. Many of the practice situations set up within the manual are expected to lead to possible disagreements, opportunities for cheating, intense competition, individual and team rivalry. It is the role of the coach to create opportunities for players to resolve these situations in a way that will impact positively upon the young participants. Without these fierce rivalries there would be limited opportunity to teach the behaviours attached to each value.

Based upon universal principles of fair play, the values underpinning the F4P coaching manual and the subsequent coaching curriculum were worked out by the Project Management team and piloted during a training week held at the University of Brighton, England in March 2004. Both document and curriculum well received as a practical set of guidelines that embodied the philosophy of the project. The document was translated into Hebrew[2] for the 30 Israeli coaches who attended. It was disseminated to community coaches on their return to Israel and re-launched with all F4P coaches, Israeli and UK, present at a training day based at the Wingate Institute of Physical Education near Netanya in July of the same year.

Having carried out extensive research in the area, as far as I am aware nothing of its kind exists anywhere else in the world. There are many sport-related community relations programmes in places such as Northern Ireland

(Sugden and Bairner, 1993) where the local Sports Council produced a 'Sport Without Prejudice' pack to encourage the use of sport to break down sectarian barriers. Sport, particularly football, has likewise been utilised in South Africa (Keim, 2003) and the Balkans (www.streetfootballworld.org). However, neither of these programmes are underpinned by a manual that develops football skills while at the same time articulating, exemplifying and imparting the qualities and values upon which mutual understanding and reconciliation are built. To this extent, both conceptually and through application, at the time of writing, the UK team believe the F4P Coaching Manual is original and unique.

A sports project designed to develop positive values is not unique. Hellison (1995) and Pratt Beedy (1997) both advocate the teaching of personal and social values through physical activity and describe their work with young people in this sphere. Whilst they both offer an abundance of valuable guidance to those coaches and teachers who are planning to explore this area of teaching, neither make specific reference to particular coaching activities in particular sports. They both offer some excellent general principles to follow many of which have influenced the writing of the manual. The F4P manual by contrast gives both a set of coaching principles conducive to values education and very specific football practices that can be used to facilitate this teaching.

It is the belief of the UK team that F4P demonstrates that — even in what appear to be the most desperate circumstances, when all else appears to be failing — if carefully designed and managed, sport can make a small but valuable contribution to conflict prevention and conflict resolution. The manual is a tangible product that not only facilitates the project work, but can also be left behind so that local coaches, teachers and community leaders can continue to promote F4P's values and principles. Sustainability is a key aim of Football for Peace. A major objective is to reach the stage where the UK coaches are no longer required and the project will be run solely by Arab and Jewish Israelis.

Whilst the F4P manual has been developed in the context of Israel's Galilee region, there is no reason why it cannot be further developed and adapted to be used in other areas of the Middle-East and further afield, in places such as the Balkans, South Africa and other seriously troubled and divided societies. In this respect, some steps have been taken to investigate the possibility of working with the Manual in the Palestinian Authority (Bethlehem and Gaza), and the International Centre for Conflict resolution based at Coventry Cathedral has already expressed an interest in utilising aspects of the F4P programme in regions of West Africa. F4P provides a framework for teaching personal values through sport that has been extensively piloted and the values that it represents are appropriate to any fractured community relations situation.

Articulating and embracing the F4P values

The values which are the foundation stones of this project were not clarified or articulated until January 2004, three years after the initiative was founded. Now they are such an important part of the project that we find ourselves referring to them in our everyday work away from the F4P context. This is not surprising as they are a set of values that clearly impinge on one's working and social life and are relevant to all citizens of any country. Listed below they are:

F4P's five principles of fair play

1. *Neutrality* —— F4P is a politics-free zone. Those who participate in F4P — players, coaches, parents, administrators — leave their political views and ideological positions outside. This does not mean changing political and ideological standpoints — this is not our business — but we do require that such positions are not expressed in and around the F4P experience.

2. *Equity and Inclusion* —— Within F4P all participants are treated equally and the commitment to equality is recognised in the way that practices and games are organised and run. Those who want to play can play regardless of ethnicity, race, religion, gender, or ability.

3. *Respect* —— The appreciation of one's own individuality and the value of others in a context of social diversity. Respect, for oneself, respect for team mates and opponents, respect for coaches and parents, and respect for the laws of the game and those that administer them are essential features of F4P.

4. *Trust* —— Players who trust one another play well together. Learning to have faith in the capacities of others to carry out their roles and responsibilities dutifully and mutually, in ways that also contribute to the well being of team-mates, is an essential ingredient of good sportsmanship.

5. *Responsibility* —— With trust comes responsibility: understanding that individual behaviour in practice sessions and in games influences and

has impact upon the performance and experience of others. Working with and for others are key aspects of F4P Projects. Success in sport, particularly team sport, relies upon mutual aid and self-sacrifice.

This is not intended to be an exhaustive list of the values that might be adopted by such a project but a set of core values which embody the spirit of F4P and best relate to our objectives.

The challenge for the coaches is to identify specific concrete behaviours that are attached to these values and to reinforce them so that they may be taken beyond the football field. To do this players need to be helped to understand what is expected of them, and one of the main tasks is to get participants to understand that in the F4P setting 'success' is not necessarily linked to the display of football skill and competitive physical prowess. Such concrete behaviours are what Pratt Beedy (1997) refers to as 'teachable moments', and I will return to them later in this chapter.

It has been suggested by some observers that the representatives of the Arab and Jewish communities should have had a greater input in the choice of these key elements of the manual. In not doing this we are leaving ourselves open to potential criticism that we are trying to indoctrinate the young people in our temporary care. That has never been an aim of the project. The values merely exist to offer those young people an alternative way of handling their choice of behaviour and to empower them in this choice. It is, however, a possible strength of the project in that it is led by a group from the UK which has no vested interest or bias towards one faction or other in the Middle East conflicts. This is something that both our Jewish and Arab partners are constantly reminding us of. Despite our financial and administrative links with the British Council, and we accept that British Council involvement may be perceived by some observers to be anything other than neutral, they have never sought to influence our work on the ground in developing the nature of the project or the working practice with the young Israeli players or coaches. In this regard we do our best to be neutral, leaving any political or ideological perspectives outside of the project boundaries. We like to think that the values that underpin the Project are not British, Jewish or Arab, rather they are universal human values. However, we must also recognise that none of us live in a cultural vacuum and we must accept that F4P is an essentially Western cultural product, albeit a humanistic one.

I suspect that opening the debate regarding the Fair Play values under-pinning the project to Israeli community leaders may have led to greater division and dissent if certain suggestions from communities had been rejected. The values are not set in stone, however, and if the manual were to be used in another context there is no reason why these set of values could not be adapted to that particular situation, whether an African state in conflict or any urban area where gang rivalry is prevalent. It is strongly felt, however, that the F4P values are appropriate and suitable for this project, and this view is supported by post-2004 research and evaluations involving Israeli and UK coaches.

Feedback tells us that football played and practised in the spirit of F4P's principles is highly satisfying and very enjoyable for everybody. Games that are most fair are also games that are most fun. F4P is a social activity requiring the development of physical and technical skills and the forming of relationships in fun-filled settings. As such, F4P projects are designed to provide the basis for lasting friendships for all involved. For this to be achieved it is important that all those who are involved in F4P — whether they are players, coaches, match officials, administrators, or parents — must accept and act in accordance with the principles upon which F4P is based. It is particularly important that all coaches endorse and embody these principles, as coaches serve as role models for the young people with whom they work. This amounts to an unwritten contract for anybody wish-ing to be involved with the F4P programme.

Delivering the programme

F4P principles of coaching

Before the children can learn, the educators must be educated. We ask coaches to coach football using a format and a style that may be alien to them. In order for them to adapt from a traditional coaching approach which has an emphasis on learning the skills and games principles of football to a player-centred approach that emphasises personal and social devel-opment, certain issues must be addressed. Soccer coaches tend, by and large, to be concerned with the teaching of skills and game understanding. They are usually aiming to improve their squad's performances in these two critical aspects of play and are rarely interested in the personal and social development of their players. School PE teachers are more likely to focus on some aspects of moral and social development but they too tend to dedicate most of their teaching time to the development of skills and tactical application. Outcome goals such as winning matches are seen as important. Performance goals such as playing the game in the correct spirit tend to be neglected or ignored completely by many coaches.

Any training of coaches that takes place, whether on or off the field, should cover the principles that are set out in the manual. The F4P manual demands that coaches adopt wholeheartedly our philosophy, approach and practice in a fundamental way which, for the majority of them, will involve a reappraisal of their practices. The project is only as good as the people who are staffing it, so a team of coaches must be recruited that reflects the diverse nature of the communities that are represented on the project. These coaches need to be open-minded, adaptable, effective communicators, have experience of teaching football and be committed to conflict resolution/ peaceful co-existence in their society. A coaching qualification would also be an advantage. It is to be expected that such people will vary in age, gender, background and vocation. Such diversity will be one of the strengths of the scheme.

It is likely that some of the coaches themselves may well be from the divided society that they are working in and may arrive with certain strong political, ideological and religious predispositions and prejudices. Although nobody is asking these people not to hold certain views, the success of the scheme depends on the assumption that any views which run contrary to the aims and values on which the project is based are abandoned, at least for the duration of the project. Anybody who feels that they cannot do this should withdraw from the project. Social cohesion between the coaches is essential and any possible areas of conflict should be avoided. Likewise any behaviour from the coaches that may undermine our stated values and serve as a negative example to those being coached must also be avoided.

An evolving pattern in the programme means that once the UK team arrives in Israel and before the commencement of the projects with the children, a day is set aside for an introduction to the project which sets out the aims and objectives, followed by some team building, problem-solving and trust games. As far as possible these sessions are organised so that the coaches who are to be working together at each venue are placed in the same social grouping. In this way, by the end of the coach training programme each cluster of coaches knows each other very well and have established a sound working relationship. Education for mutual understanding through sport is a major theme running through the F4P project and this applies to the coaches as much as the players. Once the aims and values are established and a positive relationship is cemented between each group of coaches, they then need to be trained in the most effective methods of teaching the F4P values to the young people in their care during the football project. The manual offers some strategies for coaches to use when coaching football with an emphasis on peaceful co-existence and reconciliation. The success of the whole programme is based on each coach accepting the F4P values as being of crucial importance to the project, understanding his/her role in modelling them at all times, and having the ability to recognise these concepts in action.

Conducting the sessions

The F4P values are top of the coaching agenda throughout each session. Each session is focused on a certain value, which is introduced through a **warm up phase**. This warm up does not follow the traditional format of pulse-raiser and progressive stretching to prepare physically for the activity. Instead, it includes a trust game to introduce a theme based on the F4P values, followed by an introductory physical activity, which will follow the same theme. This initial phase of the session aims to begin to break down barriers by including social interaction through problem-solving and physical contact. The 'human knot', where a team of people from different communities are linked by the hands as if tied in knot and are set the task of untangling themselves, is an example of this kind of exercise. Likewise, 'the falling leaf' exercise — one child closes his eyes and falls backwards, trusting that this new friend will catch him before he reaches the ground — is another simple example of an activity that promotes mutual aid. Trust can also be shown through 'butt stops', a simple pairs-based warm up in which one player rolls the ball towards another who is facing the opposite direction. The roller has to be trusted to call 'sit' when the ball is directly under the backside of his/her partner. If the roller gets it wrong he/she will help the partner up, and if they call it correctly they 'high-five' and move on.

During the **technical phase** of the sessions, children are introduced to a variety of collaborative skill-based practices or games. For example, the children may be asked to teach each other a dribbling skill or may work inpairs to score the highest number of ball juggles. During this phase the coach asks the players to frequently change partners, shake hands, learn names, recognise good performance with applause and share language. Working in pairs and peer coaching are crucial features of this phase designed to enable an atmosphere of mutual co-operation and warmth to be fostered across the group.

The **game phase** consists of a conditioned, modified game that facilitates teachable moments. For example, the coach might ask the group of 20 to split themselves into two equal teams of 10, numerically and in terms of ability, without any intervention from the coach. They would then play a game of 7-a-side football whilst handling their own substitutions. This process is likely to throw up issues of equity and inclusion, respect, responsibility and trust that can be reflected upon in the cool down phase.

During the skill learning and games element of the session the coach looks for teachable moments where he/she can draw attention to situations when one of the F4P values is either violated or, preferably, demonstrated in a positive way. For instance when a ball is kicked off the pitch a child from the opposite team may go to retrieve it and hand it over to his opponent: and this could be used as a means of illustrating the principle of respect. Or when the session is drawing to a close, somebody might spontaneously collect balls and other equipment and this could be singled out to illustrate the value of responsibility. These teachable moments are either addressed at the time or later during the cool down.

The **cool down phase** consists of a combination of gentle physical activities based around the values theme of the day and some discussion on the teachable moments. It should be a plenary phase that consolidates the players' understanding of the notion that each abstract value can be attached to specific behaviours and attitudes that may be exhibited in the session. It is a period for reflection and celebration of collective achievement. Ultimately, it is our aim that these behaviours and attitudes are transferred to life back in their respective communities. Our aim is to develop the shared values in all the players through competition, learning, co-operation and friendship with an emphasis on fun and enjoyment. The teaching that takes place will be based on players being able to recognise these concepts in action and learning to model them. By the end of the programme the young people involved should be able to attach each value to specific behaviours and attitudes and have the motivation to transfer these behaviours to life beyond the football pitch.

Coach and player relationships

The coach is also regarded as a role model and thus has a responsibility to display the behaviours that he/she expects from the players. Modelling is a critical aspect of this form of teaching. The UK coaches in 2004 were selected very carefully with this in mind. They went through a stringent selection process before being accepted on the training camp. One major benefit of the coach development programme was the enormous improvement in teaching techniques shown by the student coaches, most of whom were PE undergraduates training for a career in teaching. This dimension was recognised in their evaluation questionnaires which also highlighted the way pedagogical strategies were cross-fertilised between UK and local coaching teams. As illustrated in Chapters 8 and 9 in this volume, some of this cross-cultural learning is taken back into schools in the UK.

Laker (2000) defines the affective domain as a number of characteristics, attitudes and values that curriculum documents, teachers and authors claim can be promoted by taking part in physical activity. Laker (2001) recognises the development of positive relationships between player and coach as a key element in teaching in the affective domain. Hellison (1995) supports this assertion when he states that"the attitude and persona of a teacher is of critical importance to any teaching in the affective domain". Our post-project research revealed that our coaches appreciated that the work they did to show that they valued the young people in their care and therefore raise their self esteem was critical to the success of the camps. Recognition and rewards (in the form of praise and applause) enhanced the players' perceptions that the coaches valued and respected them.

The creation of what Pratt Beedy (1997) refers to as 'an environment of physical and emotional safety' is not always easy to achieve when working with two communities in conflict. It is, however, important that all children feel able to express themselves physically and verbally and to risk failing without ridicule or criticism during sessions. Each coach had a responsibility to foster a positive atmosphere through his/her manner, behaviour, feedback and influence over the group. It is too easy to allow all the good work to be undermined, for example, if the victorious team celebrates over-zealously after a game and the other team are left dejected and in tears. One F4P leader witnessed a coach dealing with such a situation on the first day of the 2004 event by using it as a 'teachable moment' and offering an alternative end to the match that left everyone's self-esteem intact. This example was discussed later by the two Arab and Jewish community leaders at the Kibbutz where the camp was based. They both agreed that one reason why both sides in the conflict are reluctant to compromise is the possible loss of pride when 'the other side' claims a victory.

The skills of observation and reflection are sometimes underrated in coaching. These qualities are crucial to the F4P coach. The coach should be observing constantly for examples of where the values are enhanced or undermined. They will then memorise those situations in order to reflect upon them with the group either a few minutes later, during the cool down at the end of the session or the following day when that particular teachable moment can be described and discussed with the group and good behaviour can be rewarded with applause and praise. An example of this was documented in one coach's diary. She asked her group to play a match without a referee and told them that they had to resolve their own disputes. She observed the chaos that followed without intervening. The anarchy transformed into collaboration as the whole group took responsibility for administering the laws of the game fairly when they realised that the success of the game relied on the adherence to rules. The coach then praised the group for recognising the importance of responsibility and respect in even the most competitive of scenarios. They had come to a realisation that compromise from both sides was necessary. The cool down provides an opportunity for the coach to ask the group to answer questions based on their perceptions of behaviour within the session. What examples of positive or negative behaviour did they pick up on? What were the consequences and the significance of this behaviour? How might future behaviour be influenced by their reflections on the teachable moment? This is something that political leaders in the region might learn from.

An action-based approach to evaluating and developing the F4P Coaching Manual

As with any project of this kind, an evaluation of its effectiveness is essential to identify strengths and weaknesses and, crucially, whether it serves its overall purpose. The F4P management team is constantly asking whether the project is making a real impact on attitudes and how can it be developed. In order to elicit some answers to these questions it was necessary to use a combination of questionnaires, observation and semi-structured interviews with a varied sample of key individuals and groups, notably the young recipients of the soccer coaching, the coaches (British and Israeli) and the sports development workers from each community. The research data linked to this paper specifically investigates the efficacy of the coaching manual. It is focssed solely on the evaluation of the manual as a document for practical use by coaches working in a football project with a co-existence/ conflict prevention agenda.

Action research methods were chosen as an appropriate vehicle for investigating the planning, piloting and evaluating of the coaching manual. Action research has been defined as defined as "a small intervention in the functioning of the real world and a close examination of the effects of that intervention" (Cohen and Manion, 1985: p. 208). Carr and Kemmis's (1986: p. 162) definition develops this concept:

> [Action research is] ... simply a form of self-reflective enquiry undertaken by participants in social situations in order to improve the rationality and justice of their own practices, their under- standing of these practices and the situation in which the practices are carried out.

They highlight two essential aims of action research as being improvement and involvement. Improvement occurs in three areas: the improvement of a practice, the improvement of the understanding of a practice by the practitioners and the improvement of the situation in which the practice takes place. Involvement runs alongside improvement, in that those involved in the practice are involved in the research process throughout each phase — planning, acting and reflecting. In the case of this study these phases are likely to be revisited at least twice over.

By choice and necessity this form of action research has been a collab- orative process which has involved a positive, constructive working relation- ship between researcher and practitioner. Henry (1986) believes that collaborative action research must involve "equality of ownership" between researcher and subject, to provide the ground for "an educative process which enables practitioners to acquire an increasing control over their professional practices" (p. 94).

There were undoubtedly some stumbling blocks to achieving the 'equal- ity of ownership' model of collaborative action research in this study. One is that the the research idea was realised in collaboration with colleagues and other potential partners in the UK. Another is that the Israel coaches and sports development teams are far away and, apart from just a few weeks in the year, cannot easily be fully consulted. Despite this, the research process and the manual that has been produced have been influenced to a significant level by all the project team and the British and Israeli coaches.

An action research approach is ideally suited to this type of work. The coaches have the degree of 'craft knowledge' to conduct the recommended practical sessions. Elliot's Cyclical model for action research (1991) can be implemented in order to evaluate the ongoing development of the manual, piloting at training weeks and its use at the F4P camps. This is a revised version of Lewin's model for action research. The coaches can become reflective practitioners who understand and perhaps question the values which underpin the way they work . This 'reflection in action', as described by Schon (1983), will lead to an analysis by the coaches of their work, thoughtful behaviour and, possibly, a change in their approach. Part of the process will be to investigate how the subjects think and the values that govern their behaviour; then to examine the beliefs that underpin their work; and finally, to offer a new way of working that may lead to change in the way that they coach and interact with the young people in their care.

Data collection process

The gathering of research data appropriate to our evaluative aims was carefully planned, utilsing a multi-method approach. This strategy is based upon the principle that those involved in the delivery of the project are its 'eyes and ears' and as such all need to make a contribution to research and evaluation. Outlined below are the main instruments through which evidence has been gathered.

1. Daily project overview and project reports. On a daily basis, each UK project leader (n=7) was responsible for holding and noting a post-coaching session debriefing with the UK coaches (n=4). He or she fed this information back to the project co-ordinator during a daily project debriefing/briefing meeting held after breakfast each morning for the duration of the project. At the end of the project each leader was responsible for compiling and submitting a Final Project Report describing and evaluating the element of the project which she or led.

2. In-depth project sampling. Key researchers were responsible for carrying out detailed observations and undertaking a series of recorded interviews with representatives of the key constituencies making contributions to the projects (children, coaches, community leaders and locally identified significant others). These recorded interviews were taken back to the University of Brighton for transcription and systematic analysis.

3. Post-project plenary evaluation questionnaires. Once the project was over all the key UK facilitators completed post-project evaluation question naires that elicit an in-depth appraisal of the manual identifying its strengths and weaknesses.

Research conclusions

The majority of coaches and players referred to the coaching camps as a very positive experience. One referred to it as 'life changing' and she on to say that "the group arrived as two and left as one. A truly wonderful experience". Several coaches commented on the gradual transformation of their group from a divided, even hostile set of young people to a cohesive, harmonious set of players prone to spontaneous group huddles, 'high-fives' and celebrations. At one project the Jewish players arrived at the Arab venue on the first day and sat as far away from their Arab counterparts as possible. By the end of the week the boys were running towards each other and greeting their new friends with a hug. One boy based at Kfar Qara said "We are always told about how different we are to the Jewish boys. I have discovered that we have far more similarities than differences".

A significant contributory factor towards the fraternal atmosphere of the project coaching group is the demeanour and behaviour of the coach. The best coaches were upbeat and positive at all times, planned appropriate, fun activities and were creative with group bonding and trust ideas. Initially the concept of 'teachable moments' was a difficult one to handle for coaches. They felt unsure whether they should address these situations spontan-eously at the time or 'bank' them in order to present them at the cool down. Eventually most decided to use a combination of both depending on the behaviour observed. This proved a difficult skill for an inexperienced coach. Observation and feedback suggested that by the end of the second day the children were beginning to understand the values being advanced by the coaches and their behaviour changed noticeably in relation to this. As the week went on coaches became more skilled in recognising 'teachable moments', selecting how best to deal with each one and using the situation to further the assimilation of the F4P values. The teaching model of 'plan-facilitate-observe-reflect' emerged as most productive in terms of utilising teachable moments.

The language barriers proved difficult for players and coaches alike. For example, some local coaches could not find a direct equivalent translation for some of the F4P values. The fact that some points were lost in translation led to a change in practice for the coaches who relied on modelling and demonstration to put their points across. Extensive use of dialogue was fraught with problems and was therefore avoided. Several of the coaches felt that their teaching skills were enhanced by this process and they are using these strategies increasingly in their work away from the F4P arena. Some of the high school teachers have incorporated values teaching as a significant part of their regular work. They had adopted what Laker (2001) refers to as 'an eclectic, philanthropic pedagogy'. The tri-lingual teaching led also to increased interaction between the three coaches who worked with each group and several coaches noted that a discernable bond had developed because of this. At Kfar Qara, for example, the Arab and Jewish coaches were setting up joint coaching sessions for the rest of the year as a result of the friendships that had developed. Language was also used to bring the children together. Coaches and players would learn greetings and football-related words in unfamiliar languages thus adding to the mutual respect theme.

The challenging nature of the teaching situation led to a minority of coaches abandoning the F4P approach and reverting to their familiar mode of skills-based, command style coaching. One coach's evaluation comments included, "I didn't see the need to keep trying to show teachable moments. It was too difficult. Instead I coached football the way I had always done at home". Whilst a certain level of sympathy should go out to a young, inexperienced coach struggling with a demanding pedagogical situation, most coaches stuck to the task, made use of the training that they had received and did eventually achieve rewarding results with the children. It is fair to say that the most proficient coaches were those who showed that they were passionate about the wider aims of F4P, modelled the values themselves on and off the field, and had been subjected to a rigorous recruitment process. There were a few coaches who made it obvious that their main motivation was to spend a week in Israel courtesy of F4P. Not surprisingly, these people tended to be either from outside of the University of Brighton where the selection process was less rigorous or had not attended the training week.

The end of project tournament received a mixed evaluation from coaches and leaders. Whilst the majority recognised it as an impressive showpiece involving 800 players and hundreds of parents and sports leaders, several witnessed the undermining of the values developed throughout the week. Some players, parents and coaches dealt with the competition in a divisive and negative way. The idea of being an honourable winner and loser was lost to some groups. Examples of this were coaches organising substitutions so that the most able players played more than the others; the children verbally abusing referees and being over-zealous in celebrating victories; and one coach recruiting strong players from a team that had been eliminated in the previous round to bolster his squad. The tournament was inclusive in that the children all received a medal. However, it was not seen as desirable by some observers for the winning team to gain trophies. Some of the UK coaches felt that a 'Festival of Football' without trophies for winners would have been more in keeping with the ethos of the project. Like it or not, competition is prevalent across not just sport but education, employment and various other aspects of life. Therefore the answer, in the view of the F4P management, is not to remove competition but to work harder on attitudes to dealing with competitive scenarios with players, coaches and, especially, parents. One suggestion from post-project evaluations is to play all games in the tournament without referees. The coaching prior to the tournament can be geared towards preparing the players' attitudes and ethics so that competitive games can take place with a minimum of adult intervention. The tournament was, and will continue to be, a rich source of teachable moments for coaches and leaders to reflect upon.

We discovered from evaluations that some Israeli coaches did not have access to translated manuals. The 2004 University of Brighton training week had prepared 30 Israelis for the project. However, these did not always turn out to be the people delivering the football activities in Israel. Many were sports development officers who managed those departments in Israel. They were often 'gatekeepers' who had to be recruited in order for projects to go ahead. It was decided that the 2006 training week would consist mainly of the young coaches who will be teaching at the camps.

Evaluations often referred to how the manual could be further developed. Some identified a need to have a two-tier set of practices as some were too demanding for the youngest players. Others suggested the inclusion of more ideas for co-operative warm ups and skill practices. Another development advocated in the evaluation questionnaires was to include more games for facilitating teachable moments and to offer suggestions on what behaviours to anticipate and look out for. One subject about which all of the coaches were unanimous was that the programme of coaching had been very effective in enhancing the F4P values with players and coaches alike. The young people directly involved in the project were extremely appreciative of the experience that they had been through and expressed some very warm sentiments both towards the UK coaches and their neighbouring communities.

The F4P manual is not a static document and its ongoing development is central to the work of the F4P management team. This approach follows the logical and cyclical model of planning-implementing-evaluating and assessing-reflecting that Laker (2001) advocates for curriculum development. As the project moves forward and we are able to reflect on the experiences outlined in this and other chapters in this book, in collaboration with The (English) FA, it is our intention to redesign the manual to improve its efficacy for our work in Israel and, where relevant, make it more widely available to other groups and organisations wishing to use football as a vehicle for overcoming serious social and political divisions in other societies in conflict.

Notes

1   The following year, 2005–2006, the Project Management Team addressed the problem of a lack of quality and uniformity in the off-pitch programmes by the development of an Off-Pitch Activity Manual to be used in conjunction with the Coaching Manual.

2   Because it is a compulsory subject in all schools in Israel, the Arabs coaches could all read and speak Hebrew therefore for reasons of cost it was not deemed necessary to translate copies into Arabic. Politically, however, for future projects it is preferable that the manual is translated into both languages.

References

Beedy. J P. (1997) Sports Plus. *Positive learning using sports*. Hamilton: Project Adventure.

Carr, W. and Kemmis, S.(1986) *Becoming critical*. Lewes: Falmer Press.

Elliot, J. (1991) *Action research for educational change*. Milton Keynes: Open University Press.

Henry, J. (1986) 'Towards an understanding of collaborative action research', in P. Holly and D. Whitehead (eds) *Collaborative Action Research Bulletin* Vol.7: pp. 93–116.

Hellison, D (1995) *Teaching responsibility through physical activity*. Champaign, Il: Human Kinetics.

Keim, M. (2003) *Nation building at play*. Oxford: Meyer and Meyer.

Laker, A . (2000) *Beyond the boundaries of physical education*. London: Routledge Falmer.

——— (2001 *Developing personal, social and moral education through physical education*. London: Routledge Falmer.

Schon, D. (1983) *The reflective practitioner*. London: Temple Smith.

Sorek, Tamir (2003) 'Arab football in Israel as an 'integrative enclave', *The Journal of Ethnic and Racial Studies* Vol. 26, No. 3: pp. 442–450.

Stidder, G and Sugden, J (2003), 'Sport and social inclusion across religious and ethnic divisions: A case of football in Israel', in Hayes, S. and Stidder, G. (eds) *Equity and inclusion in physical education and sport*. London: Routledge.

Sugden, J. and Bairner, A. (1993) *Sport and society in a divided Northern Ireland*. Leicester: Leicester University Press.

Street Football World, www.streetfootballworld.org 10 April, 2006.

Chapter 3

FROM ARMAGEDDON TO UM AL FAHEM

James Wallis

It is difficult to imagine how you will feel, even more to predict how you will react when exposed to a new and challenging situation. Whether it is trying to empathise with victims of natural disasters from the comfort of your home several thousand miles away, or fantasising about how you would cope as a golfer standing over a putt for The Open, or taking the decisive penalty to win the World Cup, the futility of trying to prepare yourself mentally for a unknown situation is immediately apparent. That is, of course, until it is delivered to your door step. The bombings in London on July 7th 2005, the same day as our impending flight to Ben Gurion airport in Tel Aviv, brought a wave of emotion and realisation to the F4P team. An overwhelming feeling of concern for my friends and colleagues who travel London transport routes on a daily basis swept across me. The irony was clear. These were the same friends that had expressed concern for my safety as the countdown to another trip to Israel approached. Even after the flood of email, phone and text communications from loved ones I am still left with a fear of repeated terrorism as the legacy of that day. The impact of these attacks might be analysed on several different levels, few of which are immediately relevant to this chapter, but they provided me with a powerful insight into emotions and events that are commonplace in Israel and accelerated my understanding of the complexities of the country and more importantly the plight of the people.

The on-going challenge for F4P as it evolves is to constantly promote its values across divided societies. Since its birth the project has expanded almost beyond control, indeed given appropriate funding its capacity is immense. However, its value to its hosts is dependent upon the extent to which it can push boundaries, raise questions, break comfort zones and in many respects challenge itself. The Megiddo, Um Al Fahem, Dalliet et Carmel project met all of these criteria. Superficial homework and close inspection of any good map of Israel could offer clues to the challenges that would confront the union of these communities under the banner of F4P. The close proximity of the Region of Megiddo and the Arab town of Um al Fahem suggests the two communities have had their share of conflict. Lands currently comprising the Megiddo area were seized by Israel during the War of Independence in 1949, forcing Arab dwellers to flee as refugees or build their own community in the far less habitable hills 5 km to the south. Located 20 km north on the fringe of the Jezreel Valley lies the other partner in the project Dalliet et Carmel. Being a predominantly Druze community, Dalliet offered its own subplot to the complex story of F4P. The Druze communities comprise around 1.5 percent of the population of Israel. Their religion is said to be similar to the Isma'ili Moslems, but little is known about the finer points of their religious beliefs as the sheiks or religious leaders closely guard the secrets of the religion, even from those who are born into the community.

Painting a picture of this particular project in many ways provides a microcosm of the wider picture: that is, nurturing co-existence between Jewish, Israeli Arab (some of which may be Moslem, some of which may be Christian) and Druze. Samir, the F4P co-ordinator of the Dalliet community, who is Druze, gave me his educated account of the path to co-existence. Even given his passion for his country and his apparent ability to speak objectively without the normal emotion and partisan stance that accompanies the majority of conversations on this topic, it was still hard to make sense of the patchwork composition of the country. In attempting to under-stand the picture I was drawn to childhood recollections of staring blankly at 'Magic Eye' posters where the idea was to focus on the mid point of the image in the hope that the Eiffel Tower or something similar would leap out at you with alarming clarity. It never worked for me. In a similar way, the closer I look at Israel and its diversity in an attempt to better understand it, the more dazed and confused I become.

It is rare that the consequences of reduced funding and leading a hand-to-mouth existence are talked of as positive, but in the case of F4P 2005 the necessity of locating teams of British coaches within the communities with which they were working was very professionally spun into a valuable innovation. Immersion into the communities was a financial necessity at the time of planning but evolved into an opportunity to catch a more realistic and enduring glimpse of Israeli life. The value to the project had immense potential as we were able to forge relationships of considerable depth — in contrast to the more superficial bonds of previous years when we would 'be at one' with the people for a snap shot of the day before retreating to our hotel, one that could have been in any Mediterranean resort.

In 2005 our home from home was Kibbutz Ga'led, located on the fringe of the Region of Megiddo, perched at the top of high ground. As the crow flies (following the security road) only 3km separate the Kibbutz from the town of Um al Fahem. The safer, more orthodox and considerably longer route would take a further 25 minutes on a good day. The message here is the need, whether real or perceived, to protect Jewish communities with no-go security zones regardless of inconvenience or the infringement of anyone's right of passage. The danger of cattle rustling and the lifting of agricultural supplies seemed to be a considerably greater possibility than anything more life threatening, but the security of a buffer between what the our guide called 'us' and 'them' did not go unnoticed.

Megiddo itself is of huge historical and biblical significance. Standing on the escarpment of har–Megiddo (literally 'the hill' Megiddo) it is easy to see its militaristic significance. As far back as 1479 BC the importance of this elevated position was recognised. Due to its strategic position straddling the main highways of Canaan and the fertile Jezreel Valley, Megiddo is widely considered to be the most fought over piece of land in the world. The extent to which control over the entire country could be established hinged on the control of Megiddo. Archaeologists there have unearthed the remains of twenty five cities representing every period of the ancient history of Israel. From its first inhabitants in the Neolithic period in the 6th millennium BC to its first recorded battle in 1479 BC waged by Pharoah Thutmose III to the British defeat of the Turks by General Allenby in 1918, hegemony over Megiddo has played huge significance in the rise and fall of empires. Possibly even more significantly, Megiddo is famous for a battle that has yet to take place, the battle to end all battles. Derived from the Hebrew word for mountain *'har'* and *'Megiddo'*, this place is better known to millions as Armageddon, the Biblical site of the final battle between the forces of good and evil: *"Then they gathered the kings together in the place called Armageddon"* (Revelations 16:16).

John, the author of the Book of Revelation, considered Megiddo as the site of the great eschatological battleground on the basis of its strategic importance and with it possession of the Holy Lands. The irony of locating a peace project in this region of biblical apocalypse should not go unnoted.

The downside of immersion into the community, and in particular a community that is striving to maintain the Kibbutz ideology of communal living, is the danger of claustrophobia. Living, eating, sleeping, breathing F4P is not on the coaches' job specifications. As a result, co-ordinating a project can raise several potential unforeseen challenges even when you feel reasonably well armed against the more predictable anxieties and occurrences. My returning coach Chris, a newly qualified PE teacher from Chelsea School, held the unenviable position of mediator between me and the coaching team who clearly did not share my sense of adventure in the concept of total immersion in the culture and the opportunities to connect with the community in order to better understand and apply the F4P message. In hindsight, their reluctance is likely to have been rooted in the need for cathartic release and a level of escapism from a highly pressurised environment. It is clear that their capacity to tolerate the social and domestic pressures of the project may have been lower than the situation demanded.

Kibbutz Ga'led is trying to maintain its traditional values but at the same time re-invent itself to support its own economy. There are more than 270 kibbutzim in Israel accounting for around 130,000 people or 2.5 percent of the Country's population. Most contemporary kibbutzim have drifted away from the anarcho-syndicalist ideals from which the Zionist movement was born in the late nineteenth century. The central ideologies of the kibbutz are self-sufficiency and communal living. Every feature of members' lives follows a communal path including meals, social activities, employment and education. Up until the start of the Gulf War of 1991 babies and young children were often brought up communally by education professionals. They lived away from their parents during the week to be schooled in the kibbutz ideology and develop a propensity for communal life. The concept here was that once born into the kibbutz you were welcomed into an extended family. Members traditionally worked within the kibbutz for the good of the community and as a result the community was completely self-sufficient and, theoretically, egalitarian. In recent years many kibbutzim are becoming more liberal in their outlook, as subsequent generations seek more worldly experiences and opportunities away from the kibbutz. It is now common to see inhabitants with vastly contrasting financial circumstances, with money kept for personal usage rather than for the good of the collective. The majority of today's *kibbutznikim* (the term for inhabitants of a kibbutz) now choose this form of communal living more for convenience and security rather than due to belief in any socialist ethic.

In order to maintain a healthy population and to generate sufficient income to keep it self-sufficient, Kibbutz Ga'led has had to evolve. The main source of income at Kibbutz Ga'led comes from the agricultural netting factory that manufactures nets for straw and hay bails. Their international exports are hugely successful and account for a large percentage of the income of the Kibbutz. It is estimated that collectively the kibbutzim are responsible for 33 percent of Israel's agricultural output and 6 percent of its manufactured goods. In this respect the kibbutz movement has maintained its importance in the strengthening of Israeli society. Those living in Ga'led are divided into members who maintain the kibbutz ideology and are fully committed to working for the common good, and non-members who are housed on the kibbutz employed outside the commune. The extent to which an individual is required to swell the coffers is dependent upon the balance between how much they consume and how much they bring in. I could not help but think that this system must surely be open to abuse: but then this is likely to be my conditioned response having being raised in a capitalist and competitive meritocracy.

Football co-ordinator for the Megiddo region and our host at Ga'led was Moti Slik. Moti was always well-presented and a man of few words: when he spoke people listened as his words were well selected and always informative. He fielded several stress-filled situations without losing his composure or self assurance. Moti had completed his compulsory military service in the 1980s during the Israeli invasion of Lebanon and in addition spent time patrolling the Golan looking out for Israeli interest in the region. The nature of his military experience is typical of the roles undertaken by civilians once they reach eighteen years of age. The structure of F4P requires each community to provide the children for the coaching days and a couple of translators to smooth communication. Moti had the benefit of knowing the youth fraternity of the kibbutz very well. His selection of Elad Mazar and Amit Sharon were in keeping with his usual quest for reliability. Both Elad and Amite were seventeen years of age and preparing to leave the kibbutz for deployment on national service. Elad had a slightly withdrawn and quiet persona but was clearly an intellectual and a valuable addition to the team. His conversation betrayed his years. It was not a surprise to learn that his most likely post on national service was regarded as the top tier of deployment — pilot school. By contrast Amit, who brought equal value, displayed an abundance of self-confidence and real strength of character, qualities which would very soon stand her in good stead in the face of considerable adversity. I was soon made aware of her ruthless streak in what I considered to be 'friendly' games of chess and backgammon (shesh–besh in Hebrew). Steely eyed and with no intention of playing the friendly host, Amit was intent on killing the game as quickly as possible with a clear sense of purpose and application of a well rehearsed game plan. The outcome of both games was inevitable: Israel 2–0 England. Predictably Amit was counting the days to leaving the security of the Kibbutz and applying her talents to the "good of her country". Despite having lived exclusively within the confines of the Kibbutz with all the trappings of a collective lifestyle, Amit was incredibly worldly-wise with strong, educated opinions and philosophies which belied her youth. She viewed national service with eagerness and a sense of pride rather than with trepidation. It is probably safe to assume that it is unlikely that this outlook would be mirrored by her generation in Britain.

My previous experiences of working with the Jewish communities have been somewhat laboured as I have often found it hard work to encourage some individuals to offer up their feelings or opinions on pretty much any political or religious issue. It soon became apparent that our presence in their homes would signal a greater degree of confidence and willingness to discuss 'highbrow' topics with freedom and honesty. As early as the first communal dinner following the first day of coaching I was asked the same question posed by my own family prior to departure, "Jim, why are you doing this?". Whether justifying your involvement to family or to hosts it is easy to understand the origin of their question and is equally difficult to answer in either direction. I was caught off-guard and unprepared to answer the more probing question delivered by Yair Sharon, Amit's father, who asked, "Do you ever feel that you are being just a little naive in thinking you can make a difference?". To that question at that time I had no immediate response.

Just 3km along the security road but philosophically a world away is the partner Arab community of Um al Fahem, a town with a population of approximately 40,000 largely comprised of four key families: namely the Mahajna (who hold the power and financial base within the town), Aghbarieh, Mahamed and Jabarean families. The town has a reputation of being a very strong Islamic community containing a powerful and radicalised

Moslem population which has long been an area of concern for the Israeli hierarchy. The location of Um al Fahem, a mere 500 metres from the West Bank, explains its strategic importance and potential for the passage of communication as well as the movement of more tangible goods across the border into and out of Palestine. Indeed the recent history of Um al Fahem provides considerable insight into the town and its political significance. As recently as three years ago the Israeli Government proposed a motion which would have moved the border between Israel and Palestine in order to relocate Um al Fahem into the West Bank. The Israeli government clearly saw this solution as an aspirin to a particularly large headache. The motion was overwhelmingly voted out by the inhabitants of the town, and even the less hard-line saw this as unappealing given the likely reduction of living conditions when living as part of Palestine. The Islamic community would have recognised this as an attempt to address the militancy of the town and its capacity to cause discomfort to the Government.

A more telling sequence of events led to the arrest and ultimate imprisonment of the then mayor of Um al Fahem, Shiek Raed Salah, along with colleagues Dr. Sulayman Aghbarieh, Mahmoud Abu Samra, Tawfiq Abdul Lative and Abdul Nasir Khaled. Collectively the group have been labelled 'The hostages of Al-Aqsa' (after the Al-Aqsa mosque which is located on the Temple Mount in Jerusalem and considered by Moslems as the second holiest site after Mecca). At no other time were opinions more polarised than when researching the imprisonment of Mayor Raed Salah. Along with being mayor of Um al Fahem, Raed Salah is the head of the northern branch of the Islamic Movement of Israel. The Islamic Movement is a series of legal political organisations representing Moslems in countries where they are considered a minority group. Having been founded in 1980 the Israeli wing of the Islamic Movement focuses on health, education and emergency poverty assistance to Palestinians inside Israel and in the occupied territories.

Differing viewpoints on the case of the 'Al-Aqsa hostages' are clearly dependant upon philosophical standing. The need to adhere to the key F4P value of political and ideological neutrality was of paramount importance when questioning members of both communities. The detention of the group had recently been extended by three months, taking the total time in detention to over two years. Mayor Salah was convicted in an Israeli court of funding the interests and actions of Hamas[1], Palestine's largest and most influential Islamic political movement. He was found guilty of accepting money from Saudi Arabia and from contacts in Iran and using a network of contacts to transport funds across the border into Palestine, thereby aiding terrorism. His legal team and his supporters maintain his innocence, citing the lack of evidence supporting the claims that money was illegally sourced from outside Israel. They also maintain that money donated by the Islamic Movement came directly from Arab businesses from within Israel. The defence team also cited the equally thin evidence suggesting the beneficiaries were in any way connected to a terrorist network. Raed Salah has never denied allegations that he has moved funds across the border into the West Bank but claims that this has been on humanitarian grounds via a system of sponsorship to benefit the orphans of the Gaza Strip and the West Bank.

By the time of our arrival Raed Salah was approaching the end of his sentence and his release was imminent. The community had been told that they could expect an announcement on or around the third week in July. A precise date, however, was not publicised in an attempt to avoid a Moslem pilgrimage to Um al Fahem or worse still a swell of militant support upon his release. The community was bracing itself for the big day sometime around the finals day of F4P, 14th July. When the finals day arrived along with a large public gathering, a procession of regional dignitaries, a host of media representatives and a huge firework display was the cue for premature celebration across the town. The phone rang off the hook and people began arriving at the stadium in anticipation of welcoming Raed Salah home after his detention. They were disappointed to find merely the culmination of F4P but would not have to wait long as they joined an estimated 50,000 others on Sunday 17th July when he was released. The crowds gathered despite the release coming one day early as an attempt to circumvent mass celebration in the Islamic communities.

The successor to Raed Salah was Sheik Hachim Mahajna. Mayor Hachim is the most likely reason why Um al Fahem showed a willingness to engage in the F4P project and to step in at short notice to donate its excellent football stadium and facilities to the showpiece finals day. It was interesting to note the existence of such a hugely impressive sporting facility alongside an otherwise typically poor Arab community. Mayor Hachim is regarded as a progressive, very forward thinking with a pragmatic approach to governance. This was the opinion of Ahmed Jabarean, our host and local project leader in Um al Fahem. Ahmed is unique. Physical features of a barrel and bright ginger hair are more akin to the front row of a Scottish rugby team than a local Arab celebrity. Indeed Ahmed himself could not recall ever meeting another ginger Arab. "I think I saw one once in Haifa," he joked when asked, "But I can not be sure." Everyone knew Ahmed. He was pivotal in the success of not only our project but also in the culmination of the finals day. He was always able to present a calm, settling exterior even under severe pressure from various sections of the community.

Taking time out from ensuring utter precision for the staging of F4P, Ahmed gave us the guided tour of the town. Immediately apparent in virtually all Arab towns is the sight of half-finished buildings, usually with the roof having been left off and with steel reinforcing rods protruding several metres from the top. Ahmed showed us his house which was no different. I enquired when the builders were returning to finish his roof. "When my sons have families and need their own home," was the reply. The reality is that the price of land is too high for the vast majority of Arabs to buy and build their own homes, plus the population density of Israel is already one of the highest on the planet. The only way to ensure a home for offspring is to build upwards. It is not rare to see three generations of family living quite literally on top of one another.

We passed numerous Palestinians who had broken the terms of their visas and had stayed in Israel in search of work. Ahmed told us the consequences of being seen talking to let alone employing such characters. It was deemed that you had subversive intentions if you liaised with illegal immigrants. He was able to show us several points of interest, not least the security road separating Um al Fahem from the West Bank. "This side Israel and good living, that side Palestine and poor living," he remarked. Ahmed told of families that were literally split by the dividing line when it was arbitrarily drawn after the six day war in 1967. He went on to describe how he himself has uncles and nephews whom he rarely sees. The passage to them, around 1500 metres if a direct route was permitted, is to drive two hours south to Jerusalem, collect relevant papers and with them permission to cross into Palestine, and then to drive to the checkpoint en route to his final destination. The process is reversed, along with rigorous security checks, on return to Israel. "You used to be able to light a cigar in your own home and walk to share it with your relative, now you would need a cigar that lasts 2 days!" The sentiment was clear but I suspect the true emotion was masked behind a smile of acceptance.

Whilst touring the town it became increasingly evident that we were witnessing a struggle within a struggle. Of course on the macro level there

is the whole Jewish–Arab / Israel–Palestine conflict but what is not immediately apparent is the extent to which a town such as Um al Fahem has
its own political and philosophical tensions, pretty much the same as all
towns and cities across the globe. Of great interest to me were images of
models advertising western products, teenage girls wearing replica
'Atomic Kitten' clothes and shops selling summer dresses that would grace
even the most quintessential English village. The message here was one that
is contrary to the popular belief, in that even in what is considered a town
with strong Islamic foundations there is a complete spectrum of practice
and interpretation of the Moslem faith. Whilst such images suggested the
community had taken the lead of the progressive Mayor Hachim, including
a more liberal outlook and acceptance of how a society may choose to evolve,
it was all the more confusing when the news broke that the F4P girls project
had been forcibly removed from the finals day in order to respect the
religious wishes of influential members of the community.

It became clear that the training day at Um al Fahem had acted as the
catalyst in the forced decision to withdraw the girls' project from the finals
day at the same venue. It was also clear that Ahmed had had his knuckles
rapped for failing to adequately prepare the religious section of the community for the huge influx of Arab, Jewish, male and female football coaches
to the stadium. The warning signs were apparent from the second day of
coaching as we packed up our kit at the training ground in Megiddo ready
to transfer it to Um al Fahem for day three of the project. (The four days of
coaching are split into two days in each community, therefore two days in
the Jewish community and two days in the Arab community.) Ahmed tried
to minimise the impact of his announcement by dropping into the conversation that Amit, our Jewish female translator, would not be able to take
part in the sessions at Umm Al-Faham on the grounds that this would
contravene the Moslem stance on the place of women and cause offence to
see men and women taking leisure in close proximity to one another. The
potential for disaster was immediately evident. If the orthodox sections of
Umm Al-Faham take issue with the work of one 17 year old Jewish translator then the presence of up to 60 girls as well as their Israeli coaches and
the female British contingent could expect to be vehemently rejected. Setting
the precedent over Amit was the key to the compromise that had to be struck
to ensure the successful culmination of the whole F4P project.

The irony of the images we had seen whilst touring the town was clear,
as was the delicate balancing act of Mayor Hachim trying to serve the

interests of both orthodox and secular sections of his community. Discussions with members of the Jewish community revealed a sense of injustice and resentment. "It is clear to me that they want to change the goal posts. They signed into F4P knowing what it entails, no one forced them on board and now they want to change the rules. They want the kudos of the event but do not want to address the issues as they arise," was the animated response of Coco, Elad's mother. "I'm not surprised," was the predictably pessimistic response of Yair, Amit's father. Of no surprise was Amit's desire to remain part of the team and to see the project come to fruition. Of greatest significance was the undermining of F4P if Amit was to remain excluded from the project on the basis of being a young Jewish female working in a male dominated space. I struggled to identify which part of her profile was most offensive.

It would not have been a surprise had the Jewish community threatened to withdraw their children from the project on the back of the exclusion of a member of their community. Although clearly disappointed, the community was keen to hold the moral high ground and preferred to take the decision in their stride. The consensus around the table was that we were welcome to try to reverse the decision but our efforts would most likely be in vain. Following a series of calls the length and breadth of the region it was agreed that Amit could continue to carry out her valuable service to the team with the proviso that she covered her arms and legs, tied her hair back and wore a hat. Amit's acceptance and willingness to confront such adverse circumstances with no thought of withdrawal again paid testament to her maturity and strength of character. Moreover the integrity of F4P and its values remained intact. With Amit excluded and then admitted back into the fold, two statements had been made:

1. F4P was determined not to compromise its values and would make every attempt to uphold its own messages.

2. Um al Fahem contained some influential and unpredictable forces that required attention in order to reduce the chances of their withdrawal from the project and their crucial support of the showpiece conclusion.

My reflections on this sequence of events revolved around the possibility of an ulterior motive. The potential of Um al Fahem testing the water with the exclusion of one female translator in preparation for the bombshell of totally withdrawing its support for the tournament was a real concern. The town's hierarchy had already cleared the way for a withdrawal by expressing concerns over the double booking of some of the facilities. It felt likely that this was another attempt by key members of the community to pressure F4P into reconsidering its choice of location without themselves having to make a difficult decision that could compromise the position and reputation of the town.

Raising the alarm on the attempted exclusion of Amit resulted in severe repercussions for the girls' project. The fallout, however, would undoubtedly have been more calamitous had there been less time to weigh alternatives and arrange a contingency. The ultimate decisions to continue with both boys tournaments at Um al Fahem as originally planned and re-locate the girls to Kibbutz Menashie impacted severely on the children, parents and coaches of the girls' project. The decision was not made lightly and there was a wide range of opinions on the stance the team should take. Some opinions were more radical than others ranging from continuing with the plan to a total withdrawal from the intended sequence of events and staging localised tournaments at a number of communities.

There was never a doubt in my mind that we took the correct course of action in upholding the request made from within Um al Fahem to withdraw the girls event from the town in order to respect the wishes of the orthodox Moslems within the community. In return, the boys could continue their big day at a premiere facility. Nothing happened on the day of the final event to suggest that my initial response to the relocation of the girls was incorrect or in any way inappropriate or even unethical. The knee-jerk reaction from some would have been to cancel the tournament and walk away from Um al Fahem, making the point that we would not compromise on our values. I could not see the logic there. It was clear that we had moved forward in the town, we had made progress merely by raising the gender question. This dilemma took us back to the ongoing challenge for F4P and the need to evolve, work outside of its comfort zone, push barriers, to ask questions, to challenge inequity. The notion of women and girls in Um al Fahem offered all of this. Reinventing and delivering the same product in moderate, progressive communities is important and highly laudable. Giving ourselves a pat on the back for this alone is not.

It was highly ambitious to expect to leave the town of Um al Fahem having delivered on all of our goals given the context in which we were working. We clearly delivered on the main rhythm of the project. The outstanding issue was whether we compromised the values of F4P by agreeing to stage

the girl's tournament elsewhere. An alternative take on this situation was to view the attempt and subsequent outcome as a success in putting the status of women on the agenda. We had made a challenge to the position of women and raised a sensitive issue. What is more, it was clear that we had generated considerable waves and had certainly challenged ourselves in the process. Given the timescale and timing (Mayor Salah *et al.*), it was a lot to expect broad acceptance of male and female coexistence in a very public leisure pursuit. However, looking at the glass half full, the main issue and central theme of F4P, that of coexistence across ethnic diversity, enjoyed almost uninterrupted success. Viewing Um al Fahem as a 3 or 5 year plan and slowly pushing the gender issue is a more constructive and realistic way of advancing the notion of equity than taking a poorly considered emotive response that would be damaging to the long term strategy. Lose the battle, win the war.

The future of F4P is clearly dependent upon the value attached to it by those controlling the purse strings of organisations which have a vested interest in the advancement of co-existence, the education of the younger generation or the development of football. F4P has the capacity to continually add value to all three of these dimensions if any long term assurance is forthcoming. Reflecting on the questions and controversies thrown up by the Megiddo–Um al Fahem–Dalliett et Carmel project it is clear to see that F4P is not going to die waiting. Numerous issues have been opened, questions raised, and debates are still rumbling along. There was little sense of closure or completion. Indeed Moti, the football supremo of Megiddo, has taken steps to initiate his own girls project following his perceptions of F4P. The fireworks to mark the culmination of 2005 may as well have been a celebration to mark the opening of the 2006 project, given the speed with which attention turned to evaluation and statements of intent for the future.

In situations where the picture is constantly changing it is prudent to pause a while and take stock of how and whether objectives are being met. Whether to take a step back and amend the picture accordingly, to retreat to replenish physical and mental reserves or merely to appreciate the scene of what has been created, it should be considered good practice to build-in time to regroup and take an objective view. Recollections of such quality time during the project offered up several emotions and even moments of clarity. The first and foremost point of concern is the experience of the children and whether the F4P product/message/theme is being served up and whether it is coming to life. The success or failure of F4P is in many ways measured by the impact it has on the behaviours of children. In our time in Israel we have a limited window of opportunity to make these assessments. We get a snapshot of the climate which we are pivotal in creating. Our anecdotal evidence from the multitude of shared experiences across 18 communities and 1,000 children says little of the longer term impact of F4P. The question of sustainability and regular co-existence projects is one for the future. The presence of a strategic approach to researching the impact of F4P has allowed the practitioners to make their own judgements based on observations of their coaching sessions. What we see is in many respects the extreme opposite of how football has moved at the elite level. We can look to anecdotes of individuals in the professional game who suffer from 'White Line Syndrome', where crossing the line onto the football pitch is the signal to trade every ounce of socially acceptable behaviour for cheating and vulgarity. F4P is the polar opposite as it starts by affecting the social norms, casting them all away as children cross the white line onto the pitch. This is the theory as well as the reality. From where I stand, on the side of the pitch in a militant town on the fringe of the West Bank it is the reality, at least for the short term.

A second recurring thought concerns the position of the parents of the children who willingly allow their children to engage in the project. Each time discussion is raised on the difficult position of parents, memories surface of an emotional exchange between John Sugden and the father of child who had enjoyed the 2004 project. The father had been caught up in a suicide bomb in Afula in 2001 and had lost his sight and his career as a surgeon. He had asked his son to guide him to John to thank him and give his seal of approval to the project. In conversation with a parent from Ga'led she revealed that it was difficult to think of anything else while her son was at the project in Um al Fahem. She signed off by asking us not to underestimate the trust that parents are showing F4P and that even considering taking a busload of Jewish children to Um al Fahem is something to be proud of and not to be taken for granted. The same mother would reiterate this point later in the week when we needed consolation after it became apparent that the girls project was under threat due to tensions within Um al Fahem.

It is difficult to measure effect. Perhaps the only real way of judging the success or failure of F4P is on a personal level. For any given child, the evidence — through observation of their behaviours towards one another and the 'feel good factor' emitted from each group as it tried to untie a human knot, choreograph a goal celebration or huddle up at the start of a game — was compelling. On reflection, the response to Yair Sharon's question of our possible naivety that our presence could make a difference was now clear. F4P has shown it can make a difference on the human level to the values and experiences of the children. It can help to put issues onto the agenda in communities and encourage them to think about whether and how they address key values. The ultimate decision may be taken to reject sentiments raised but raising the issue; opening up the forum is an important process.

On the issue of making a difference on a wider national or political scale my attention is drawn to an enduring image on the western edge of the har–Megiddo settlement where someone felt the need to place a two metre high fence post. Inscribed down the length of the post is the writing "May peace prevail on earth". This seems a small, almost insignificant statement in the middle of the most fought over piece of land in the world, but perhaps a fitting metaphor for Football4Peace?

Note

1   Hamas became the governing party in the Palestinian territories after winning the Palestinian election in February 2006.

Chapter 4

FROM KFAR KARA AND MENASHE TO ACCO: A COMPARISON OF TWO FOOTBALL FOR PEACE EXPERIENCES

John Lambert

"I am very bad man" said Yusuf. It was 16th July 2004 and he was gazing over the football fields in Barcai, in the Menashe district of Galilee. There could hardly be a better metaphor for the state of Israel than the setting for the football club. It is flanked on one side by the Kibbutz Barcai where in 2001 a Palestinian from the West Bank had broken security and shot a resident in her home. On the other side the field was overlooked by the watchtower of a heavily-protected Israeli Defence Force camp, and to the East, barely a few hundred yards away, was the Muslim town of Qazir where the aforementioned gunman was holed up for a while after the attack before being captured by the IDF (Israeli Defence Forces). Yet, with all this symbolism for conflict around them, young children from both sides of the sectarian divide were playing football together with an unbridled enthusiasm, supervised by Arab and Jewish coaches, all fully committed to peaceful co-existence. When I questioned Yusuf about his statement of self-disapproval he explained that the atmosphere created between the boys of his town of Kfar Kara and the Jewish Menashe district had been "very beautiful" and that he and his fellow Sports Community leaders should be facilitating this kind of co-existence activity all year round instead of relying on the visit of the UK Football for Peace group.

The 2004 project in Kfar Kara and Menashe exceeded expectation in terms of the enhancement of the five F4P values and the development of positive community relations. The values that underpin Football for Peace — respect, responsibility, trust, equity and inclusion and neutrality — were fully embraced by all participants from day one and were modelled on and off the football field. It was my third year of involvement with Football for Peace. The 2004 project held particular importance for me in that it was the first time that the F4P Coaching Manual, of which I was the lead architect, would be put into practice in the field. Being based in a new project in an area so close to the West Bank was a challenge that I found both a source of excitement and apprehension. As it turned out, due to the work of the local people and the UK coaches, the project was a resounding success.

How do you measure success in a project that aims to enhance co-existence and conflict prevention through sport in a divided society? Firstly, the effect that the values-based coaching had on the attitudes of the children was gradual and progressive but was there for all to see. "They came as two and left as one", commented Esther, one of the UK coaches, referring to the children from the Arab and Jewish communities. These communities were less than five miles apart but few of the boys taking part in the project had ventured into their neighbouring towns before. Their mistrust of strangers was manifested in the initial reluctance of the children to mix with each other on the first coaching day. The contrast between that day, when the two groups sat on opposite sides of the pitch staring at each other until the UK coaches eventually persuaded them to sit in mixed teams, and the final day when the players and coaches of both communities greeted each other with spontaneous hugs, 'high fives' and handshakes, was both unforgettable and very moving, even for this cynical old football coach. The second indicator for success is whether the working relationships built between the respective sports leaders and coaches from both communities is sustainable. All empirical evidence points to a development of links between Yusuf and Heim (from Kfar Kara and Menashe respectively) and their sports development teams that have lasted at least until my visit in July 2005. This has included joint coaching projects and matches, not to mention a genuine personal friendship.

So what were the significant components of the 2004 Menashe/Kfar Kara project which made it such a positive experience for all involved? The genuine commitment of the sports leaders and coaches towards peaceful co-existence was a crucial element. Both communities were represented at the training week in England in March 2004 and had embraced the values that underpinned Football for Peace and the philosophy behind it. One abiding memory of that week was the bus journey to London Stansted airport on the final day when Nestor, the Menashe Sports Development manager, instigated an impromptu and joyful Jewish and Arab singing and dancing festival in the aisle of the coach. As the guys danced between the seats Nestor told the Arabs to make the most of their fun as, unlike the Jewish members of the party, they were likely very soon to be strip-searched by El Al security at check in! A joke appreciated by everyone which, I suspect, would have been neither uttered nor appreciated at the start of the team-building week for fear of upsetting sensitivities and causing offence. There is no doubt that lasting friendships based on mutual respect were forged over that week by the sea in Sussex.

The core F4P values of respect, neutrality, equity and inclusion, trust and responsibility need to be not only accepted by the local and UK coaches but modelled by them in situations on and off the field. This approach was epitomised by Yusuf, Nestor, Heim and their community sports colleagues in 2004. A charismatic and strong project leadership in each Israeli community is essential to deliver the necessary resources, organisation and support locally in a country where political and social tensions can undermine even the most benign enterprise. For example, engendering the co-operation of the local football clubs is one task where these leadership skills need to be put into play, as we will appreciate later in relation to Akko 2005. Recruitment of a group of Israeli children and coaches that reflects the diverse religious and ethnic population is also dependent on the local community leader charged by their local council and the Israeli Sports Authority with the responsibility of leading the project.

Another characteristic of a successful project is recruitment of UK coaches with sound teaching skills and personal qualities that will allow them to adopt different, and in some cases, unfamiliar coaching styles in order to facilitate the programme in the F4P manual. For the effective use of the manual F4P coaches must be confident and skilled enough to move away from traditional command teaching styles to practice guided discovery and divergent methods in order to allow 'teachable moments' to be exhibited by the children, and for the coach to observe and reflect upon them. There were some excellent examples of this in Kfar Kara/Menashe 2004. Chris, a University of Brighton student, for example, recounted how he was brave enough to set his group up into a game with no referee and sit back to watch the ensuing anarchy. "I was very worried about what might happen without an intervention from me. What did happen, after some arguing and conflict at the start, was a recognition by the kids that without them showing each other some mutual respect and having to compromise, there could be no game". All coaches were put through a training programme, in the UK and Israel, where coach education focused on embracing the F4P aims and values, and modelling them. They were shown practical examples of values-based teaching in action. The majority, like Chris, were, to their credit, willing and able to leave the relatively 'safe' skill-based pedagogy behind and adopt this new holistic view of teaching.

My involvement in the Football4Peace programme in Kfar Kara/Menashe 2004 convinced me that values-based sports coaching could make a tangible impact on community relations in societies where divisions exist. It is a programme that could have generic use across a variety of situations. It is supported by a dedicated coaching manual and has been piloted in one of the most socially, religiously and ethnically divided nations on earth.

With the always happy, often very heart-warming and sometimes quite emotional experience in Kfar Kara/Menashe to look back on, my new challenge in 2005 was to oversee the creation of a similar coaching programme in the ancient city of Akko. The main body of this chapter, therefore, consists of an assessment of the Akko project in 2005, a comparison with the experience in Kfar Kara/Menashe and an evaluation of the efficacy of using the F4P coaching manual in this multi-racial, urban context. The final section will review the project in Akko as a whole, draw comparisons with other projects and identify some of the lessons learned.

Some people, from outside of the F4P management group, had questioned the choice of Akko as a location for the project. After all, it is widely regarded as a city where Arabs, Christian and Muslim, and Jews, including immigrants from all over the world, live side by side in relative harmony compared to other cities in Israel. Is it a divided society and, if not, why is a co-existence operation required there? The F4P management group's initial meeting with the Akko Sports Authority in November 2004 convinced us of both the desire from the city to be part of the scheme and the need for its inception there. As it was to be the first urban venue for F4P and a major site for the research programme, assuming the management of Akko project from a UK perspective was an interesting prospect for me. An extensive research programme was to be conducted in July 2005, involving structured interviews and observations which would reveal some interesting insights into attitudes and policies in 'the city of harmony'. As others have found in places like Northern Ireland, we were to find that under closer examination the social and sectarian geography of the population is not always what it first seems, and that the reality of community relations did not always match the rhetoric. This situation proved more apparent as the week progressed.

Lydia Hatuel, the Head of Sports Development for the city council, had been delegated responsibility for leading the operation locally. She was an ex-Olympic fencer, now in her early forties with three children, belonging to a family with a fencing tradition that originated from Moroccan Jewish immigrants. Her athletic zenith had been an eighth place finish in the Los Angeles Olympics, the middle one of three trips to the Olympic finals with the Israeli team. One sensed that her status in the city had been enhanced by her background of athletic achievement, and that it had opened a few doors for her. As Sports Development manager, she was entrusted with the responsibility of organising F4P in Akko. 'Role overload' is the type of term that I try to avoid using but it could definitely be applied to Lydia. She owned three mobile telephones and it was not uncommon for her to be using them all simultaneously. She was late for everything and in a constant state of 'crisis management'. Her mitigating circumstances were that she was also bringing up three young children — evidence of which was the condition of her car, the interior of which could be politely described as 'lived in'.

Lydia's assistants were Benny and Heim, two men who had clearly not used their athletic prowess to advance their careers. They were both rather rotund men for whom jogging once around the circumference of a football pitch would be a challenge. Their role seemed to be to transport the UK team of five around various beaches when we were not working. Due to the security situation these beaches were two parts holiday resort and one part prison camp. Argaman beach had a combination of sunbeds and cocktail bar alongside armed guards and barbed wire. Other leading characters in the Akko project were Adi and Lelakh Telem, two sisters who had completed three years national service and then moved back home with their parents. They had been recruited to be co-ordinators of the Akko girls group which travelled to Tiberias for their coaching. Their secondary role was to act as our guides around the historical sites by day and the social scene by night.

It was the Telems who greeted us on our first day in Akko. They took us to Kibbutz Masaryk which was to be a very comfortable home for our six day stay. That evening Adi and Lelakh took us to eat some falafel and then for a social drink in Nahariya, a seaside resort that could easily have been in Florida but for the men with guns and bomb detectors that greeted you at every entrance. Whilst relaxing in a beach bar with the waves lapping in barely ten metres away, our hosts were giving us their perspective of modern Israel. Lelakh described how she loved her country but felt the citizens of Israel were living on borrowed time and on how Sharon had been voted in because like a big fat, favourite uncle he made them all feel more secure. Both the Telems had an engaging frankness about them and asked questions of the UK students with a bluntness characteristic of Israelis. Their time in the army had given them an outer toughness which was reflected in their complete independence. Lelakh said that she was happy to live in a flat below her parents and had no desire to enter a relationship which involved mutual dependence. On her only trip to England she spent two weeks following the band 'Beautiful South' on tour which took her not to London but to Derby, Hull and Swindon. The highlight was meeting the lead singer backstage in Middlesborough. That sort of eccentricity is, in some ways, quite appealing and rather English. She had no career but relied on casual work when she needed money. They both had their beliefs about how they wanted to lead their lives and were not going to be unduly influenced by external pressures. This resolution, often in the face of vehement opposition, seems characteristic of both the Jewish Israeli and the state that they inhabit.

Later I asked some questions about the organisation of the project in Akko and, in particular, the equipment available. There were no satisfactory answers forthcoming from either of the Telems. Lydia was not present or available to give us details of venues and equipment. It was at that point that I, for want of a better phrase, 'smelt a rat'. We were due to begin coaching the following day and we had no idea of what pitch we were using, what footballs and other equipment we had and, most importantly, how many, if any, children would be attending. My anxieties proved to be well founded when we met Lydia the following morning and discovered that she herself had no answers to the questions.

Coaching day one at any of the eight project venues would have been predictably chaotic but nothing like the mayhem experienced at the Hapoel Akko ground. The day started well with breakfast at Kibbutz Masaryk, followed by an informal planning meeting on sunloungers by the pool. The UK group were joined by Dekel, Mahmood, Ahmed and Liad, some of the young Israeli coaches that we had met on the training week in England. These four lads were to be the shining lights of optimism amid the prevailing murky cynicism surrounding the project in Akko. They were all in their late teens, Mahmood and Ahmed from Arab Muslim families and the other two from Jewish immigrant backgrounds. Liad's family, of Moroccan descent, lived and worked on the Kibbutz donating a sizeable percentage of their salaries to the commune in return for a peaceful, secure existence. These young men all played for the Hapoel Akko youth football team, were good friends and immediately connected with the UK student coaches. After an epic Israel v. GB aqua-basketball game (narrowly won by the visitors), we met Lydia for lunch. Following further unfruitful discussions with her about equipment over an omelette sandwich, it was decided that the British Council offices in Tel Aviv should be contacted in order that somebody bring a supply of balls, bibs and cones to the Hapoel Akko coaching pitch that day. As leader of the project, I tried not to convey my anxieties about the logistics in Akko to the four young, enthusiastic UK coaches in my charge. Caroline and Lewis from the University of Brighton, Julian from Liverpool John Moores and Steven from St Marys London were beginning to ask the questions that conscientious young teachers would ask such as, How many children will there be? What equipment will I have? What area will I be working in? The fact that I had no answers to these basic questions signalled to them that there might be trouble ahead.

The signals emanating from Lydia and her team of assistants had warned me that the start of the project in Akko would be a difficult one. I was not wrong. We were greeted at the ground by a representative of the local football club who seemed surprised that we needed any equipment at all. Following some negotiations, I was able to gain access to four balls, ten plastic cones and one set of bibs. The number of young people that attended was disappointing — barely half the number expected. Nevertheless, a ratio of one football to eight players would have meant that any coaching from the values-based manual would be impossible. Fortunately, in the nick of time, our supply of equipment arrived from the British Council in Tel Aviv, which allowed the coaches to at least follow the programme that they had trained for. However, only two of the expected eight Israeli coaches had arrived to act as translators and offer support. As a coach of twenty five years experience, I was ready for the feeling of anti-climax but my young UK coaches, who had prepared for three months to make their small but significant impact on conflict resolution in the Middle East, were visibly deflated.

We had no alternative but to soldier on regardless. However, the first session, so important for building positive relationships between the children and the coaches, was undermined by lack of resources and local support. Without adequate translators the relevance of the coaching activities was lost on the children and they became restless, and in the case of a minority, unruly. This was hardly surprising as they had paid 200 shekels to attend a soccer camp run by English coaches which, they believed, was to improve their soccer skills. They did not expect to be taking part in team-building and trust games run by coaches whose language they could not understand.

At the stage when Lewis, Steven, Caroline and Julian set about firstly attempting to control, then teaching their groups, I observed from the periphery whilst connecting with a few of the local people who watched from behind the metal security fence that surrounded the pitch. Noticing a group of four Arab boys closely observing proceedings, I approached them and, using the man accompanying them as my interpreter, asked them why they were not taking part in the football. They told me that they had wanted to but their parents could not afford to pay. These lads, part of the under-privileged Arab community, were just the type of people that the project should be targeting. Bizarrely, due to a locally imposed charging policy, they were part of the constituency of young people excluded. Where was the equity and inclusion here? Taken aback by the fact that the children were being asked for money, I sought confirmation from Suzin, mother of one of the Jewish players. She explained that several families had been prevented from sending their children by the 200 shekel fee asked. She added that she believed this sort of activity to be very important to the future of her community and that she was delighted to bring her son along.

The issue of charging children to attend was a major controversy in the context of Football4Peace. The Akko Sports Department had received generous funding, a sum of five thousand shekels, from the Israeli Sports Authority in order to set up the project. Where had this money gone? It had not been spent on equipment or coaching/translating support. Indeed, against the wishes of the F4P management team, the Akko Sports Department had raised extra money from the children and their families by asking them to pay. It betrayed a lack of trust which angered Ghazi of the Israeli Sports Department who had set up the link with Akko. Lydia initially denied that fees were paid, contradicting herself the following day by saying money had been collected, and on the third day, during the PR visit of the manager of Akko Municipal Council, she claimed that the money had been paid back to the families. The UK coaches made their disapproval of the pay-to-play policy very apparent to Lydia and the four Arab boys were permitted take part in the football for the rest of the week.

Lydia accepted that access to the F4P event for children had been a problem and recognised that more Moslem schools should have been used as recruitment grounds for Arab children. Whilst the range of children that attended broadly reflected Akko's population as a whole, nearly all of the children were players at the Hapoel Akko Football Club which inevitably meant that they tended to be socially integrated middle class kids who were familiar with each other anyway. Many of these boys behaved in a way that suggested that they could benefit from some values teaching but by not mixing them with a significant number of representatives from the minority groups in Akko, for example new Russian immigrants, we seemed to be defeating the object of the exercise. If these conflict prevention and co-existence projects are to serve their purpose, more careful recruitment of children must be a priority.

Akko was represented in the girls' project based in Tiberias but some girls had obviously missed out. One such girl was Nili who was watching the action on day two at Dromi field. When quizzed about her non-parti-cipation, she lamented the fact that, although football was played by girls in the Jewish schools, there was little opportunity for girls within community football clubs and that these male-dominated institutions, like Hapoel Akko, tended to exclude female players. Akko had, to its credit, agreed to recruit girls to the all-female project and to host some coaching. Unfortunately, this enterprise was also riddled with mismanagement. The girls who visited Akko for coaching sessions were expected to play on the beach. Whilst this would cause no problem if kicking a beach ball around for ten minutes, working intensively for two hours in 35 degrees proved, not surprisingly, to be impractical. The girls from Saknin and Tiberius insisted that the coaching be moved to their fields. It was representative of the status of women's sport in the area and of Lydia's lack of influence that no grass area could be found for the girls to play in a town of the size of Akko.

It was Hapoel Akko Football Club who had insisted that we use Dromi field that day so that their teams could train at the main stadium. The Dromi arena was a rutted, barren plot of land with a dilapidated, rusty goal at each end. It would have been condemned as a health and safety hazard in Britain. The fact that their visitors, who had travelled from England to run coaching courses for their children, were banished to such an unsuitable venue was not untypical of the attitude of the club towards Football4Peace and it demonstrated a lack of respect towards the UK team. The day at Dromi was poorly attended as it was out of town and, therefore, inaccessible to the families without a car. Lydia's relationship with the local football club is strained to say the least. This is not helped by the fact that she is a female in a very patriarchal domain. When questioned about the effect that gender has on her role in Akko sport she used the term 'gender war' to describe the efforts of women to have any impact on decision-making and roles of power in Israel.

The explanation offered for the non-appearance of Dekel, Liad and several of the other young coaches on day one of the project had been that they were told by their team coaches from Hapoel that attendance at their training sessions was compulsory irrespective of other commitments. Due to a clash of times with their co-existence coaching these young men had split loyalties. In March we had flown these five young people from Akko to England, trained them for a week to teach football and provided them with a sightseeing programme. Five British football coaches had flown (on the day terrorist bombs had sent London into chaos) to Israel in order to coach local kids in a co-existence project at the expense of the British Council and the Israeli Sports Authority. Hapoel were effectively, by pressuring the young lads into attending a pre-season fitness session, depriving us of translators and, therefore, undermining the whole F4P programme. In the context of the preparation work that had taken place, this was irresponsible, dis-respectful and indefensible. It showed complete recalcitrance towards all five of the values that F4P is based on. What ensued was a rather unsavoury power struggle between Football4Peace, represented ineffectually by Lydia, and Hapoel Akko FC with Dekel, Mahmood, Liad et al. in the middle. Being a woman in the predominantly masculine enclave of Israeli football, Lydia's influence over this situation was always going to be marginal.

That morning the young Israeli pawns in this particular chess game of sports politics had been persuaded that their commitment to F4P was of greater importance than attending a 3000 metre training run set up by Adam, their coach, and had agreed to attend day two of F4P at the Dromi. Adam, as their coach, was an important figure to them and had a significant influence over the boys. He had persuaded them to agree to miss day one of the project but the young Israeli coaches could also see their wider respon-sibility of their role in F4P. The coaching session that evening, despite being played on a surface that resembled an army missile target area, was pro-gressing well. Scanning the four groups and observing the children visibly engaged by the young coaches, I spotted what I assumed to be Adam appearing at the entrance. This was going to be a seminal moment for F4P Akko 2005. The characteristic of Adam that I remember most vividly was that he was huge. As he strode purposefully toward me I was bracing myself for a possible physical assault. It seemed like he took an age to walk across the field and when he eventually reached me he said tersely, "I need the boys to come to a training session". I explained that I, as a coach myself, could to some extent empathise with him but, for all the reasons that had earlier been given to the lads, they needed to be with the project. Adam accepted the situation reluctantly and walked away. Some of the Hapoel coaches watched the coaching that week, including two who had helped out with translation on the first day, but they mostly stayed away which was in stark contrast to the Kfar Kara/Menashe experience the previous year.

Later that evening the UK visitors were invited to a barbeque at the house of Liad's family, the Boskelas, which was in the Masaryk kibbutz. These delightful people, originally from Morocco, provided us with a cold beer, lit the barbecue and showed a genuine interest in our work. Being billeted in the community was an innovation introduced to the 2005 project by financial necessity. In the past the whole UK contingent of coaches, leaders and researchers had stayed in a large hotel in Nazareth. Due to budget tightening this had not been possible in 2005. Living in Akko for a week in a small group of five enabled us to develop a close working relationship with each other as well as our hosts. It also allowed us opportunities to gain an insight into the rich social and cultural mix of the Akko community which provided a valuable research opportunity. Why, for example, had Hapoel Akko FC shown themselves to be, at best, indifferent and, at worst obstructive, about our visit? Adam's arrival at the barbeque offered the opportunity to find out. My discussion with Adam enlightened me as to why we had not received the support expected from HAFC. Discussion is not the correct term as it suggests a two-way interaction. I remember listening for long periods without contributing very much to the discourse. The picture that emerged was of a group of proud coaches who were very committed to working with their young players and, because they were not adequately briefed on the visit of the UK group, were resentful and dismissive. Adam was defensive about his status in the football coaching community and unjustifiably attempted to question our coaching credentials. The lesson to be learned here, and illustrated by the Kfar Kara project, is that all partners have to buy into a community relations project both mentally and physically. Lydia and her team had not engendered support from HAFC and this had impacted on every aspect of the project. In 2004 everybody in Kfar Kara/ Menashe had been pulling in the same direction under strong leadership and the contrast was marked.

Under close examination the sectarian geography of Akko is similar to that found in a divided city like Belfast. Whilst the range of ethnic and religious groups may be wider in Akko there are large areas that are almost exclusively Jewish and Christian Arab, and substantial Arab Moslem-only districts. The Druze and Baha'is are other significant minority population groups in the city. The non-Jewish citizens add up to approximately 28% of a total 45,000 inhabitants. An example of the multi-cultural nature of the population is that of the four Jewish coaches only one of their families was from Akko originally. Anton's family were relatively recent immigrants from Russia. Since the collapse of the Soviet Union, Russians by a significant margin have provided the greatest number of immigrants into Israel and Russian is effectively the country's third language. Whilst Anton seemed very settled into Israeli life, he explained that there had been some backlash aimed at Russian immigrants who are accused by a minority of Israelis of using a very tenuous Jewish identity in order to escape a harsh regime and become economic migrants. In effect they were accused by some of exploiting the 'policy of return', which provides a home in Israel for all those of a Jewish faith from around the world: a legacy of Zionism and a by-product of the persecution of Jews across Europe.

It is hardly surprising that there is a complex weave of cultures existing within Akko. Since 1504 BC, when it is said to have first been inhabited under the Egyptian Pharoah Thutmose (after his defeat of the indigenous population at the battle of Armagedon), this strategically important Middle Eastern port has been occupied by a long list of different civilisations from the ancient Egyptian, Crusader, Mosem-Arab and Ottoman empires. Testimony to this turbulent history are the archaeological remains, examples of which are the vaulted halls and fortifications which were built under the occupation of Richard the Lionheart and his crusader army, and the Al Jazzer Mosque erected by the Turks in the late 18th century. As we toured the ancient city on day three Adi and Lilaque were our companions and guides along with Veled, mother of Ahmed, one of our coaches. It was as usual, however, their casual asides that gave the most interesting insights into the Israeli psyche. Describing the events at the parallel girls project in Sakhnin, the Telem sisters, who were helping out as translators, commented on how they had been appalled by the attitude of some of the Jewish girls who refused to share the bus with the Arab girls from Sakhnin because they 'smell'. The Telems had attempted to diffuse the situation by quietly pointing out that after playing football for two hours in 35 degrees it is inevitable that all the girls would perspire and that the alternative to boarding the bus was to walk home the hundred miles back to Akko. The Telem girls' conflict prevention skills were tested to the limit that week.

As we were viewing the remnants of Akko's volatile history I was struck by the amount of graffiti and garbage around the architecture. Lydia later commented that this was typical of Arab neighbourhoods and that, whilst most of the Arabs living in the city adopted a modern, educated approach to life, many had yet to learn civilised practices that involved respecting their environment. According to her, the Arabs wanted the money and status that went with positions in local government but did not address their civic responsibilities. She told me that, although she voted for a different party to Sharon, that all parties shared the aim for separate states. "They want to work here and then bomb us", she observed. She then added, to offer some balance, that there were some issues of inequality and that Akko had a good record of peaceful co-existence. The Israeli characteristic of being outspoken and very transparent about their views makes them a very effect-ive source for informal research material. Hearing some of these 'off the record' comments did beg the question; why has a person with such disdain for some sections of the Akko community been selected for such a pivotal role in the project?

The coaching had become progressively more successful each day as the practical logistics had been addressed. Day three had most of the elements that are required to make F4P effective; namely equipment, trans-lators and children. There was a fight between two of the boys which was precipitated by a parent shouting from behind the security fence. It is usually behaviour on the pitch that incites violence on the terraces, but not in Israel. As I moved to instruct one of Lydia's assistants to eject the guilty spectator from the ground I was approached by first Veled, who invited the UK team out to dinner with her family, and Suzin, the mother of one of the Jewish players. Suzin had heard that the tournament on the final day was scheduled to be played at Um Al Fahem, a Moslem town close to the West Bank, and that it was rumoured that the Jewish boys playing there were being subjected to stone throwing. Reassuring her that this rumour about stone throwing was completely fabricated, I asked her what the source was. She had been told by another of the parents who had been warned herself by somebody from Akko. Suzin turned out to be a Jewish mother with a progressive outlook who had very natural concerns for her child's welfare. She told me how valuable it is for these kinds of community relations activities to be set up for the young as they are more receptive to change. She also confirmed that her son had understood and enjoyed the football-related values education sessions. Suzin would send her son on the bus to Um al Fahem which reflects a commitment to co-existence on her part which is quite something when you consider that the town is regarded as the radical Islamic capital of the Arab community within the state of Israel, and not a stone's throw (if you pardon the expression) from the Green Line (the border with the Palestinian Authority).

That evening the Abd Elhady family collected us from the Kibbutz to take us out to dinner in two cars. Both rocked to the sound of modern Arabic dance music and travelled well above the speed limit. Being familiar with Arabic hospitality, it was no surprise to see that what seemed like the whole menu had been ordered and served on our table. The UK coaches, being used to a basic 'student' diet, were amazed by the variety and quantity of food available. Our hosts apologised for the lack of alcohol and insisted on paying the bill. We could see that, whilst they were not a poor family, paying the bill for 12 people would make a significant dent into their weekly budget. Nevertheless, you offer to pay your way but you do not argue over Arab hospitality. As we walked to the cars Veled told us that we should all go to the beach at Nahariya. Her husband started the car but before heading off he paused, walked to the rear of the car and opened the boot. He passed a large bottle of Heineken to each of the UK coaches and then opened the bottles using the buckle on the seat belt before driving us to Nahariyya. We spent a rather bizarre but very enjoyable East meets West night sitting on the promenade enjoying a cold beer whilst the Abd Elhadys drank cola, played music and chatted. At one stage their daughter gave us an informal Arab dancing lesson accompanied by traditional Arab music which emanated from the portable stereo unit that sat next to the cool box holding the drinks. We headed back to the car at approximately 3 am. That night the students, having been subjected at home to images in the Western media of Moslems being mainly violent extremists, had been introduced to a warm, friendly family who, although devout followers of Islam, are accepting of and welcoming towards people from all other faiths. This widening of experience, and therefore perceptions, is invaluable in the fight against prejudice in society and an important feature of F4P.

Breakfast time came and went the following day. We emerged closer to midday and took a dip in the pool to clear our heads. The regular daily evaluation meeting took place a little later than usual. Although all three of the UK coaches had attended the training week, it was interesting to hear how effective the coaching manual had been for them out in Israel for the first time, particularly in relation to handling the concept of teachable moments. As explained in Chapter 2, teachable moments are the situations that occur within the session where either positive or negative behaviours in relation to the F4P values are exhibited by the children. For example, a child may accidentally trip an opponent in game, stop, help the opponent to his feet and collect the ball for the free kick. This would be registered by the coach and banked so that it could be highlighted during the Cool Down phase to reinforce the values of respect and responsibility. After early teething problems, they were now well immersed in the coaching so were able to offer the author of the manual some feedback on its efficacy in the field. Progress in embedding the values of F4P in Akko had been slow. Some of the children had not been briefed about the rationale behind the coaching, were impatient when values rather than football were being discussed and were behaving in a disruptive manner. A couple of the coaches had found that observing and reflecting upon the teachable moments had been very problematical for them. They had found the tri-lingual situation difficult and that several of their group were very resistant to the aspirations of the project. These coaches had found themselves reverting back to a traditional command coaching style with an emphasis on skill development. It is, to a certain extent, understandable that coaches might take the 'safe' option when challenged by such a difficult situation.

The success, however, of the values-based approach to coaching sport is dependent on coaches being confident and skilled enough to adopt a divergent teaching style which might involve very little coach intervention. Effective organisation, observation and reflection skills are required in order that the teachable moments can be facilitated, banked and recounted during an evaluation period. An example of this might be to ask a group to set up their own game, pick equal strength teams, organise their own substitutions and referee themselves. A coach can then stand back and observe teachable moments covering equity and inclusion, respect, responsibility, trust and neutrality. This will be followed by a period of reflection where players are invited to evaluate their behaviour in relation to the shared values of the project. Recruitment of coaches with the commitment to this style of coaching and an understanding of a more holistic approach to teaching is important. It became obvious that a small minority of coaches on the 2005 project had no intention of adopting a new approach to coaching sport and these, it emerged later, had not been subjected to as rigorous a selection process as some of the Brighton University students. A manifestation of this reluctance to embrace the F4P values and ethos was the over-zealous attitude of these coaches, and consequently their players, to winning matches at the end of project tournament. Coaches with a humanistic outlook towards teaching, like those in Kfar Kara in 2004, gain a great deal of reward from the way, as Esther put it, they had seemed to have "'changed attitudes and, in some cases, changed lives".

Given the circumstances in Akko, progress was understandably slow. The UK coaches were advised to ensure that all activities were presented in a fun way to win back the goodwill of the children and to forget the development of football skills in favour of personal values. Research information from interviews conducted in Akko over the final two days of the programme revealed that the children understood and had seen the need for the teaching of the five core values. Several admitted that it had changed their attitude to other children; some said it had not. The coaches, without exception, ended up as converts to the use of sport as a tool for the teaching of values stating that they had plans to integrate it into their physical education lessons back in the UK. PE teachers have always seen themselves as teachers of moral and social education through physical education. However, when questioned, few could explain how and where they plan for this, and how success can be measured in this area. The National Curriculum for PE in England and Wales (2000) refers to the development of personal values through PE but offers few guidelines on how this is to be delivered or evaluated. If the 100 plus PE teachers and coaches from the UK who so far have passed through Football for Peace disseminate strategies from the F4P manual and encourage the teaching of values through sport it will have left a useful legacy at home as well as in Israel.

Over the final two coaching days some of the children showed that they had grasped and, in most cases embraced, the values being taught through the football sessions. This had seemed very unlikely at the beginning of week and credit for this, in no small way, should go to the young coaches from the UK and Israel who, in a world where headlines involving youths are usually negative, were outstanding role models. An unforgettable example of this was when, after one particularly competitive game ended, one team were celebrating victory very loudly and the losers were very sore about their defeat. Dekel spent some time emphasising the need to generous in victory and defeat with your opponent. He stressed that both teams should firstly shake hands after the final whistle and respect their opponents. He later confided in me that he felt that one reason why the Israelis are reluctant to give concessions to the PLO is that this is always followed by partisan victory celebrations in the West Bank which most Jews find difficult to tolerate.

The tournament on the final day at Um el Fahm was followed by a banquet that was arranged in order to bring all those working on Football for Peace 2005 together in an informal, social celebration. Before entering the restaurant the young UK coaches based at Akko said a sad farewell to their Israeli counterparts. There was a certain irony that, whilst the five UK staff were enjoying the hospitality on a table with Lydia and her two sports department assistants, Dekel, Liad, Mahmood and Ahmed were on their way back to Akko with fifty children on a bus. Lydia had only three comments to make on the finals day; not that 800 Arab and Jewish children had played together happily in a joyous celebration of Football for Peace, but that the Israeli national flag was not displayed, that the police presence was too low key and that she was unhappy about Veled attending the banquet without being formally invited (the same Veled who had worked tirelessly unpaid all week to help make our stay a happy one). Lydia had often given the impression that her sole motivation for being part of the project was that it was what she is paid to do.

So, what lessons had been learned from the Akko? Certainly the main ingredients of a successful project where the objectives of peaceful co-existence and conflict prevention through values-based sports coaching are met can be identified as follows. Firstly, that a fertile coaching environment where all local participants are unified in their genuine support of the project, both logistically and philosophically, needs to be created. Each of the F4P values will have a set of specific attached behaviours which should be modelled in all situations by coaches and leaders. Secondly, a robust and carefully planned recruitment of both local coaches and children so that the coaches are genuinely buying into the spirit of F4P and the children represent the constituency of people that F4P is aimed at. Thirdly, the recruitment of UK coaches who are fully committed to the principles of teaching values through sport and to the adoption of a divergent, 'light touch' coaching style that is pivotal to the success of the F4P manual. The 2004 project in Kfar Kara/Menashe had these essential ingredients and the consequences were quite stunning — a truly spiritual experience. If one or more of these pre-requisites — is missing, as in Akko, then the product is rather unsatisfying and falls short of being the flagship community relations scheme that we are striving for. In fact, failure to address the above considerations can lead to F4P itself being a source of conflict. The F4P values contract had been fully embraced by the splendid young coaches of Akko but had been regularly broken by their community leaders. As the Manager of Akko Municipal Council said on his visit to the project, "Mistakes have been made but we must learn from them and put them right for future years".

Chapter 5

FROM NORTHERN IRELAND
TO NORTHERN ISRAEL

Michael Boyd

I was asked to take part in Football for Peace (F4P) by Shane McCullough, a Sports Studies lecturer from the University of Ulster, Jordanstown, early in June 2005. Many years ago, Shane had been a student of John Sugden, the co-editor of this book and coordinator of F4P in the1980s and 1990s. John had lived and worked in Belfast and had organised community relations sports programmes for Protestant and Catholic children during the 'troubles'. His idea was to recruit student volunteer coaches and a leader from Northern Ireland because having people involved who lived in another 'divided society' and were experiencing a maturing peace process, would give F4P an added dimension. I have known McCullough from my days as an IFA (Irish Football Association) Coach working in the Mini Soccer department. I suppose you could say I was a late substitute for Shane who, for family reasons, pulled out at the last minute.

Until this point I had not heard of Football for Peace. Once I had given it some thought and carried out a quick internet search on the project, I realised it could be a great learning experience, which could have a serious impact on the project I manage in Northern Ireland for the IFA called the Football For All (FFA) project. As Head of Community Relations at the IFA I have managed this project since February 2000. Initially formed to address sectarian incidents at Northern Ireland internationals, FFA has broadened to include challenges of racism and making the game more widely inclusive, particularly of women and people with disabilities.The FFA project is all about working in partnership with the football family and I am responsible for the equity training of IFA staff, promotion of good relations with supporters and community outreach initiatives.

My F4P project diary

July 7 2005: major terrorist attacks in London. So far 37 dead and 8 bombs, the radio informed me as I started the trip for F4P. At Belfast International Airport I met the other three Northern Irish people travelling to take part in F4P. Thankfully I already knew these three students from my work at the Irish FA. Heather McCracken is a very proactive student who had volunteered on FFA and plays for a local Women's team. Both Conor Lynch and Gerard Boyle are Irish League footballers who had coached with me in China on the University of Ulster's high profile Culture Kick programme in May 2005. We left Belfast International to fly to London Stansted with some trepidation. It was a very scary time to be travelling to London. The irony was not lost on us: it used to be those who flew into Belfast who were fearful for their welfare. At Stansted we met some of the English people taking part in the project who, like us, were somewhat apprehensive. We had the necessary ordeal of passing the security desk in the airport. The Israeli woman at the security check point checked my passport and realised I was from Northern Ireland. Then she said to me in earshot of one of my new English friends: "These bloody English just don't know how to deal with bombs. It is easy for us my friend. It is normal!".

I smiled awkwardly and nodded politely. I thought it wise not to challenge this woman as she has the power to stop my new adventure before it has even begun. Once we had passed her I apoligised to my English friend, saying I felt the comment she made was out of order. Bombs and terrorism are not normal. Given the timing of her comments I felt quite disgusted by what she said, but felt some empathy. Having been brought up in Northern Ireland in the 1970s and 1980s I had become almost immune to the madness going on around me. Sectarianism, fear and violence were a normal part of everyday life where I grew up in East Belfast. Unfortunately bombs, shootings, beatings and murders were regularly on the news and the troubles scarred my life.

The next day, July 8, after the 5 five hour overnight flight to Tel Aviv's Ben Gurion International Airport, we arrived at Kibbutz Givat Haviva at approximately 10am where we rested and prepared for the training day due to take place in Um al Fahem the following day. Givat Haviva was chosen because, even though it was a Kibbutz — and by definition very Jewish territory — it had earned a reputation for being a centre for co-existence-related education and development.

Our first team meeting was at 3pm. Ground rules were set and there was a warm welcome from our hosts. As a late addition to the project team I had missed the training event held at the University of Brighton earlier in the year and this was the first time I had a real chance to come to terms with the project, its schedules and expectations. My first impressions are good. I got the sense that this is a very positive project in which I felt proud and privileged to be taking part. In particular I was intrigued by the values-based coaching manual. I thought there was potential to have a similar coaching manual introduced in Northern Ireland for cross community coaching and I looked forward to seeing this values-based coaching in action. I am told I am leader of the Nazareth-Nahalal group and this fills me with a sense of pride and excitement. I got to know my team of coaches quite quickly and they seemed like a great group. I read all of the information given out so far and I lookied forward to the challenges that lie ahead.

The following day, July 9, was very interesting indeed. We had a lecture in the morning to recap the principles of the coaching and the main thrust of the tournament. Then we headed to a training pitch to go over the coaching sessions highlighted in our F4P manual. This was great fun but I failed to grasp what our instructor was doing other than demonstrating basic coaching. There was no meaningful content with regard to value-based community relations objectives other than "high fives" and lots of other somewhat trivial points of physical contact. Of course, given that football is by tradition quite aggressive and competitive, this is hardly surprising. The feedback I got from my team suggests the instructor did not emphasise the trust building/community relations element of the coaching enough. This had been instilled in a training session earlier in the year in Brighton which, due to my late addition to the project, I had missed. I felt somewhat disadvantaged as I presumed this is when most of the groundwork was carried out to get the coaches and leaders to buy into the principles of F4P. However that said, I felt there was real potential in the coaching manual and I looked forward to seeing it in action once the project-proper starts. I have confidence in my team!

In the evening once the training was concluded we were taken to the Jewish community, Nahalal, where we were to be hosted for the rest of the project. Nahalal is a Morshev, which is similar to a Kibbutz insofar as it is a community of members with some shared community facilities, but differs from a Kibbutz to the extent that each household earns its own wealth and controls its own domestic economy. Our host gave us a tour of the area and made us a wonderful barbeque at his home. It was fantastic and our first real insight into Israel. However, as is ever the case in divided societies, the version of history that you get depends often depends on the identity politics of who you are listening to. Our host is Jewish and some of his comments I felt were quite biased against Arabs. I immediately recognised the compar- isons between Catholics and Protestants back home. It is obvious there is a power struggle going on and the issue of identity is very much in focus. He mentioned a few things which made me uncomfortable but I did not get into a debate with him and instead listened intently. The issues are complex and deep rooted, again very much like home. I think it is often a wise tactic to keep your mouth shut and listen when you are ignorant of all the issues at hand.

Sunday July 10 and the real work begins! We started the coaching this day and this is really were the project gets going with regards to trying to make a meaningful difference to the children. Jewish and Arab children are brought together through the medium of football and the Coaches have to work hard to bring to life the values that underpin the F4P coaching manual.

We brought the children together and I made a short speech on the basic principles of F4P. In doing so I became acutely aware of how much was riding on our local friends who were given the task of acting as interpreters. Somehow I did not really feel their hearts were into the principles of F4P. I later found out the interpreters we had did not have any training in F4P (they too had not attended the Brighton training event) and the principles we were trying to get across did not come naturally to them. As you can imagine, given the circumstances in Israel, there was some initial mistrust between the coaches and interpreters from different backgrounds. For example our Jewish coach felt it was very important to inform me early on that the Arab coaches and players were very aggressive and violent. I told him that I would make up my own mind on people and asked him to concentrate on helping my team of coaches get their messages across to the children in their charge.

The coaching, given the poor standard of the pitch and communication problems, was of a very good standard and I was proud of my team. Their heart and soul was in it even if they were let down by the poor attitude of some of the interpreters. Right from the first day there was a real feeling of mistrust between our two interpreters, one Jewish and one Arab. I had a quiet word with both of them to reinforce why we were all there but I am not sure they grasped the concepts of F4P and, more importantly and depressingly, they did not seem to want to.

The following day, July 11, in the morning we visited the River Jordan and Sea of Galilee with our Jewish hosts. This was quite simply amazing and spectacularly beautiful. I have always had an interest in the area since I studied Religious Education at school and I found the whole experience very uplifting. According to the New Testament, most of Jesus's miracles were performed in this area where he preached as a young man and the Sermon on the Mount took place in a natural amphitheatre on a hillside overlooking the sea — which is really a large fresh water lake.

Into the second day of the project and the coaching went really well with the children starting to mix better. As a team we had decided to emphasise the values of trust and respect at every opportunity. One of the Israeli coaches warned us there was 'big tension' in the community at this time, as the result of a bus bomb. Nevertheless, the children responded enthusiastically to tasks that there were given to do — although what their thoughts and deeds were outside of the project were hard to ascertain. I was pleased that our team had really emphasised the values of trust and respect during the coaching and at the end of the session I praised my team for the work they had put in and told them I felt they were really making a difference. I explained to them that we had a real responsibility to emphasise to these young people and the adults that football, when well managed, could be used as a vehicle to promote respect for difference. This trip was not really about the football, it was about providing a positive space for these children to play together and break down some of the barriers they had in their minds about each other. If we could challenge one young person in our group to think differently and to question their own stereotypes and prejudices the trip would be worthwhile.

July 12 and in the morning my religious education continues as our Arab hosts give us a tour of Nazareth, the highlight of which was a trip to the Basilica of the Immaculate Conception. Built to commemorate the Virgin Mary's motherhood of the Baby Jesus and his boyhood in Nazareth, inside and out the Basilica is breathtakingly beautiful. Nazareth is a beautiful, bustling, noisy place full of exciting markets, brilliant colours and equally evocative smells. It is an Arab town with a majority Moslem population, but with a large, mainly Orthodox, Christian minority. High on the hill north of the town is the other Nazareth, Nazareth Illit, a large Jewish settlement which characteristically looks to be more prosperous and which declined the opportunity to take part in F4P.

The people are very friendly towards us and before coaching we are treated to another barbeque. We are beginning to learn not to devour the early courses too ravenously as the food just keeps coming and coming until, just when you think you cannot eat another mouthful, they bring out the main courses which inevitably consists of trays of mouth watering kebabs on long sword-like silver skewers. In particular I am struck by the similarity between our Arab and Jewish hosts. Hospitality from both was excellent and there appear to be more similarities between both than differences — a scenario which again reminds of the Catholic and Protestant divide at home. In my experience once you get past the fear of difference there are often more similarities than distinctions between people. This is a lesson I have learnt many times working not just with Catholic and Protestant children in Ireland, but also with footballers with disabilities.

For some reason today the coaching was not of a very high standard. I blame myself for this as the team had poor preparation. This lack of preparation is my fault as I had agreed to too many offers from our hosts to see the local sights. I don't regret that decision though; it is not too often you get to explore such a beautiful and exotic place. And anyway, in this culture it is extremely bad manners to turn down hospitality. I discovered later that this was a problem that had affected other projects. Achieving a balance between our hosts' traditional obligation to lavish hospitality and the logistical and practical needs of the project is an issue which the F4P management group will have to address.

In Nazareth the pitches we are forced to coach the children on are in extremely poor condition. This was mainly due to localised political disputes between the town officials and Sports Director who were involved with F4P and the local football club who, unlike in previous years, chose not to make their excellent facilities available. Despite the difficult conditions I am very pleased that the team still reinforced all the principles of F4P with the children. Feedback from the team suggested that the children were continuing to come out of their shells and I make a mental note to myself that this is a very worthwhile project. As I look around the pitch I start to see friendships blossoming between Arab and Jewish children who most likely would never have had the chance to meet if it hadn't been for

F4P. This fills me with a great deal of satisfaction that we are actually making a real difference.

In the evening we had a collective UK coaches dinner in a Bedouin-style restaurant in central Galilee. It was great to catch up with all the other people, especially Conor, Heather and Gerard from Northern Ireland. I got a chance to speak with Elana Budwig from the British Council and I was immediately struck by the commitment she has to promoting positive community relations in Israel. Our chat filled me with more enthusiasm for the remainder of the trip and even for my work back home. I think Israel is a place with massive potential for creative projects that are designed to promote positive community relations, and the Government there should think of more ways to support such projects. It made me think of how lucky we are in Northern Ireland to have organisations like the Northern Ireland Community Relations Council and Equality Commission. I believe community based projects are often the pillars which can carry peace forward. Israel is crying out for such projects. However, I have to remind myself that it took many, many trouble-filled years and a maturing political peace process before such large-scale initiatives began to take shape in Northern Ireland. F4P is but one small step along this arduous route.

After dinner the F4P Coordinator, John Sugden, called the coaches together and highlighted an emerging problem that, because of religious interpretations, some local people had with the girls playing their tournament and final at the same place as the boys. A lot of the leaders were unhappy but it was decided that the girls would play their tournament and final at a different venue and join the boys at the end for the presentation of medals. I had no problem with this but kept pretty quiet at the meeting as feelings were running high and I did not want to upset people. At the end of the day you have to consider the culture and environment we were working in. To go ahead and ignore the concerns and fears of the local people would be a massive 'own goal' as far as I was concerned. F4P is very ambitious and I believe the project made a very positive impact on all the people who witnessed it, however, it is a delicate flower and it would not take much to undo all of the good work done by offending local sensibilities — particularly those rooted in religious principles. When we got back to our community I had an informal chat with my team about the issue for the girls. I was taken aback by the mature attitude my team took. Afterwards I reflected on how much my own team of coaches had matured on this trip.

I was very fortunate to have such an intelligent, experienced and principled team around me.

In the morning of July 13 we had a leaders meeting to discuss tournament planning, transport and equipment. At this meeting it was decided I would have to simultaneously manage a couple of teams at the tournament as the girls having a separate tournament meant that coaching personnel was stretched. I was delighted by this turn of events as it meant I would experience some more 'hands on' coaching, giving me the opportunity for reinforcing F4P's values with new young people. After almost a week working with them, I also had more than enough confidence that my team of coaches had the ability to work on the day unsupervised.

In the afternoon the coaching was superb. My team was back to top form and it was obvious the children were having fun. Most importantly it was clear the children were continuing to overcome stereotyping and prejudice to form new friendships. I hoped in my heart these friendships could be something more than 'holiday romances' and perhaps they could plant the seeds to overcome the problems these young people faced routinely throughout the year.

In the evening our Arab hosts took us out for dinner and an impromptu party. This turned out be a late night and was great for further team bonding among ourselves and with our hosts. At the party we learnt a great deal about how our Arab hosts viewed Jewish people. As had been the case on the first night in Nahalal, I picked up on a lot of bigoted and highly politicised comments. It demonstrated to me just how much of a divided society we were living in. Mistrust and bigotry followed us into both communities but the fact that, despite their obvious prejudices, the people from both sides of the divide were willing to support F4P filled me with hope for the future.

July 14, the day of the tournament! As a PR exercise, the tournament and especially the award ceremony were a great success. With regard to the principles of F4P, however, it nearly undid all the good work that was carried out during the week. Throughout the week we had constantly bombarded our children with messages of peace, trust and respect. The tournament sent out the message to everyone that winning was all that mattered. I know this was not intended but unfortunately tournaments with big award ceremonies tend to have this affect on people. It was not so much the children who caused problems, but some the local coaches and other adults on the sidelines who became far too competitive — a picture sadly repeated on any given Sunday morning in any youth football league, in the UK at least. That said, it was a great showpiece and very well organised.

I was given the job of managing two new teams during the course of the day and had to split up physical fights between Jewish and Arab children from the same team twice. I found this very disheartening. It was hard not to get caught up in the desire to win during the tournament day and in many ways it really was a big success. In particular I was very impressed with the standard of football being played. However, that said, the reason we were all there was to promote positive community relations through football and it was my opinion that the tournament did not help us do that. The success of this high-profile tournament was the public relations value it provided for potential funding agencies and The FA. I understand this is necessary to secure the funds to make the project work, but more thought must be given to this part of the programme for the future.

It was good to see The (English) FA representatives at the event. One of them, ex-professional footballer Brendan Batson, refereed one of the finals. Brendan had been one of England's first black professional footballers — with West Bromwich Albion — and subsequently had done a lot of anti-racism work in football in the UK and elsewhere. F4P's aims and objectives resonate with efforts made by The Football Association to help their Israeli counterparts to develop strategies for combating racism and sectarianism in Israeli football, which is why FA are supporting Football for Peace.

After the awards ceremony all the coaches and leaders were brought together for yet another barbeque. It was a great way to relax and reflect on the tournament. All the coaches at my table agreed the tournament had been great fun but had not moved the project forward in terms of making more of a difference to the young people involved. The interesting thing was that some of the coaches were clearly upset by the experience of the tournament and angered by how competitive it had all become. I think this demonstrates how much those coaches had bought into the principles of F4P. That night, well after midnight, we collapsed into our beds totally exhausted.

The day after the tournament, July 15, after a good breakfast we set off for a feedback session in the Druze market town of Dalliet a Karmiel. This was a useful exercise as it is important to get feedback as early as possible from the local and UK coaches. It was clear that the majority of people who spoke considered F4P 2005 to have been a huge success. However the problems and difficulties faced were highlighted and noted. Hopefully this will have the effect of making F4P 2006 even better than 2005.

After lunch we set did some shopping and haggling in the local Druze market. This was a fun experience and allowed us to snap up some bargains for our family and friends back home. I now have a delightful tablecloth all the way from Carmel on my dining table in sunny East Belfast! It was exhilarating to be reunited with all the other coaches and there was a great party atmosphere as we headed for Negev for some camel riding and tracking exercises. This was a great experience. We danced in a Debki dance lesson and partied into the early hours before sleeping under the stars in Bedouin tents in the desert. That is not a regular experience for me but one that I enjoyed immensely! Truly unforgettable.

July 16 and after breakfast we set out to travel to a Dead Sea Hotel. A number of us visited the Messada ruins and found the whole experience very interesting. It was a great way to relax and take in some of the local culture. I then fulfilled a dream of going for a swim in the Dead Sea. It was another wonderful experience to add to the many I had on the trip. In the evening we let our hair down, partied and celebrated F4P 2005. It was a late night and very enjoyable. The next day, a little fuzzy-headed, we set off after breakfast for the airport and the long journey home. It had been an amazing trip and one of the most fulfilling and enjoyable of my life.

Reflecting on F4P 2005

Looking back on the F4P 2005 experience there are a lot of positives that spring to mind. There was a very high standard of coaches and leaders who were shown a lot of trust to deliver the project on the ground. There is no doubt in my mind that the team did deliver all they could in 2005.

If I had to be critical of the F4P 2005 experience I would make the following points:

1. It was too ambitious with too many coaches and leaders. A more focused team working in one area would make more of a concentrated and long lasting impact.
2. As a whole the tournament itself did not live up to the guiding principles of F4P. It became more about winning than celebrating co-operation and co-existence.
3. The local people should be more involved in the design, delivery and monitoring/evaluation processes of F4P.

I would like to see more time spent with the local people in Israel listening to their fears, concerns and ideas for F4P. A smaller team could spend a month working with members of the British Council, local coaches and interpreters to lay the groundwork for the project. This period is vitally important to allow the local people to buy into the principles that underlie F4P and to take ownership of the project. In my opinion the project will make much more of a sustainable impact if it is delivered by local people on a cross-community basis. This could be monitored by a small team from the UK and British Council. It is important to find a suitable place/space to carry out the work of F4P, somewhere with good pitches and also lecture room/class room facilities. The good work that is within the coaching manual could also be brought to life through other mediums perhaps even using art and music. Highly trained community relations facilitators could be brought in to work with the young people to explore identity, prejudice and stereotyping in a non-threatening and fun manner.

In Northern Ireland we are blessed to have some excellent people working in the community sector who could be briefed and utilised as facilitators to activate the young people involved to respect difference and promote understanding. If the young people could be brought together on a residential basis this would be more beneficial to the development of the work. Over two to three weeks a youth forum consisting of young people could be brought together to discuss the issues facing them and the impact they feel F4P is making. The forum would have to be well managed at first with contract agreement by the young people to promote trust and understanding. This contract would act as a safeguard to help move the forum forward. With the help of the British Council we could set up regular focus groups with the young people involved to monitor the impact F4P is making.

A Football for Peace Advisory Panel could be set up to oversee the development of F4P 2006. This panel could have representatives involved in the promotion of positive community relations through sport.

There is massive potential for F4P 2006 and I would love to play a part in it. With the permission of the University of Brighton I would like to use the Value-based Coaching manual used in F4P to develop a new coach education course in Northern Ireland that could be used by Coaches looking to promote positive community relations through sport.

Conclusion

F4P 2005 was a success and the potential for F4P in the future is massive. The work of F4P builds upon the experiences of similar schemes and projects in South Africa and Northern Ireland in that it seeks to make grass-roots interventions into the sport culture of Israel and Palestine, while at the same time making a contribution to political debates and policy development around sport in the region. There is absolutely no doubt in my mind that F4P 2005 provided an opportunity for social contact across community boundaries in Israel. This is a major achievement that should not be skimmed-over or overlooked. This is key to the success of the project. It is obvious that a lot of planning and expertise was utilised to make the project so high-profile and successful.

Central to the success of F4P is the promotion of mutual understanding. The coaching manual and coaches played a key role in making this happen. Success in communicating understanding of the coaching manual is very dependent on the interpreters and local coaches. Unfortunately the interpreter and coaches working with me had not experienced the UK training week and came 'cold' to the idea of the values-based approach to coaching. This had a negative impact on our work initially, but as the week developed we made real progress with the local adults involved in the delivery of the project.

Sustainability is a key issue facing the project in the future. It is my feeling that more effort needs to be made here to ensure ongoing cross-community contact. More emphasis could be placed on the empowering of local people to run F4P which would allow for more of a lasting impact. Obviously this would have to monitored by a select F4P team. The ultimate success of F4P would be that one day the whole project was run by local coaches in Israel in partnership with the British Council and University of Brighton. Maybe one day, just like it turned out in Northern Ireland, F4P could make a significant contribution to making sport in Israel a key area in the struggle to find a lasting peace.

Chapter 6

MAAGAN AND THE GERMAN DIMENSION

Gary Stidder

Introduction

This chapter seeks to assess the effectiveness of one project in the Northern Galilee region of Israel and view this through the eyes of the volunteer coaches who took responsibility for implementing the F4P curriculum. This chapter pays particular attention to the experiences of one member of that team who had been part of F4P since 2003 and had returned to Israel in subsequent years for other projects. What is different about this individual is that he is German and it is hoped that his perspective may enable the reader to view the community relations and co-existence project from a non-UK perspective.

This project was somewhat different from the other projects, which tended to pair distinctive Jewish and Arab communities, in that it involved two different Arab communities and various Jewish communities. The communities had participated in the 2004 project and for the 2005 project worked in partnership in establishing a project site. Each of the participating communities were within thirty minutes drive of each other and were located primarily on the shores of the Sea of Galilee. Emek Ha Yardain is a Regional Council made up of small Jewish communities and includes Maagan, Kinneret, Afkim, Ein Gev, Dgania, Neve Orad and Alumt. El Battouf is a Regional Council made up of small Arab villages including Mashad, Uzar, and Romany. Tuba Zangaria is an Arab Bedouin village in northern Israel and it is located near the Jordan River. Bedouin society is distinctive within the wider Arab community. In Israel 70,000 Bedouins make up the population, twenty per cent of whom live in the Galilee region of Northern Israel. The vast majority of Bedouins in Israel have long given up their traditional nomadic lifestyle and now live in small settled communities. The village is surrounded by Jewish cities and is therefore one of the only Arab villages in the area. There are 6,500 people who live in Tuba and most of them make a living in commercial activities. A village populated by the Bedouin tribe of El Heib, Tuba is situated near Kfar Hanassi and overlooks the Jordan River. The tribe settled in this area at the end of the eighteenth century and until the 1960s lived in tents and shacks. Today, visitors can see traditional lifestyles set in a modern town.

The coaching team consisted of a UK leader, a German exchange student, an Irish female undergraduate PE student, one female and one male UK postgraduate PE student. We all were billeted at the Kibbutz Ashdot Yaacov approximately fifteen minutes by bus from the project site of Maagan. The dynamics of the coaching team were such that there were two experienced coaches who worked closely with the other three. Like other project sites, each community had recruited children between the ages of ten and fourteen. The project site in Maagan accommodated one hundred six children who would work in two particular age groups: 10–12 and 13–14 years, who were mostly boys but also included eleven girls.

UK coaches perspectives

During the course of the project the UK coaches made a number of observations regarding the commitment of the respective communities and the way in which they had embraced the F4P core values. Of particular note was the way in which both the Jewish and Arab coaches had adopted the Football for Peace philosophy and the ways in which they had incorporated this in their approach to the coaching. One of the coaches suggested that this was not only a surprise to them but was also very reassuring:

> The main thing which I have been surprised about is how well the Jewish and Arab coaches actually get on with each other. I have nothing but pure respect and admiration for them in terms of their commitment to this project and their strong desire to make it work. It amazes me that some of the coaches have even taken time off work to get involved in this. (Extract from UK coaches journal)

As the project unfolded there were a number of incidents that highlighted the value of the 'teachable moments' which were an inherent part of the football for peace coaching manual and the overall curriculum (see Chapter 2). Several UK coaches had recorded such incidents in their journals and suggested that within the context of their coaching this had helped them to instil the main purpose for being involved in the project:

> I had an incident when we were playing 'stuck in the mud' which was a real break through as in order to win they had to work as a team to help save each other and to begin with they were not doing it at all. After I stopped them and spoke about team work and working together as one they were completely different. They were going out of their way to help each other and were not just helping those who were from their own communities. (Extract from UK coaches journal)

> I had a teachable moment where one of the boys wouldn't participate because I would not let him work with his friend all the time. We then sat down as a group and discussed why we should try and work with others and how it makes others feel if you refuse to work with someone. After this everyone was much more receptive to each other and were more prepared to work with a variety of people in the group. (Extract from UK coaches journal)

During the course of the week the issue of competition arose as each group prepared for the planned tournament on the final day which would bring together all the boys and girls from various projects that were taking place. In this respect, the UK coaches were generally consistent in their views in that any issues of cultural difference had little or no bearing on any tensions that arose from over-competitiveness during the small-sided games sessions that they took part in. For example, one of the coaches recalled:

> My general opinion about both my groups was that they did not ever argue or disagree with people because they were either Arabic or Jewish, but more because of the competiveness. This was parti\\cularly the case with my older group where they were all predominantly from the same community and had grown up with each other. They would be very competitive in games just like normal kids would at school and would say similar kinds of things to wind each other up. (Extract from UK coaches journal)

The project at Maagan culminated in the preparation of the children for a final tournament and involved the UK coaches talking to them about the concept of fair play and sportsmanship. During the course of the week a number of girls had participated in groups alongside boys with the full consent of both parent and community leaders. The project also had female translators, coaches and community assistants who worked happily alongside each other with both the boys and girls in their respective groups. On the final day, however, the project team had learnt that the girls would not be permitted to play at the intended venue and would have to participate elsewhere in a separate competition away from the boys who would play their final at the prestigious Peace Stadium in Um Al Fahem. This news was not well received by the girls who had practised and competed with the boys throughout the week and been part of the group's development, and even resulted in some girls withdrawing from the activities on the penultimate day as a form of protest. One girl in particular sat out of the football training and expressed to her female coach and translator her feelings of disgust, indicating that she felt offended and insulted by the decision to exclude the girls. These feelings were later passed on to the UK project leader and highlighted the extent to which this had been completely counterproductive in promoting the aims of the project.

> She has trained with the boys all week and now she is told that she must join the girls from the all girls project and cannot play with her team that she has a strong team relationship with. This is not only detrimental to the project but goes against everything we stand for and value. (Extract from UK coaches journal)

One of the female UK coaches reflected upon this and expressed her level of disappointment as well as offering some insight into the situation.

> I was completely disgusted when we were told that the girls could not attend the tournament and had to go somewhere else. I was later told by one of the Israeli coaches that she had one of the girls come up to her and ask why they could not play at the Peace Stadium. She also asked why we had lied to her by saying that when we all wear our t-shirts it's a sign of neutrality as this was clearly not the case. When I heard this it almost brought tears to my eyes through frustration and feeling like we had completely failed. I was completely gutted.(Extract from UK coaches journal)

The German dimension

Since 2003 the Football 4 Peace project had been able to recruit a number of University students from institutions outside the UK. One of the universities with whom the UK management team had established links was the German Sports University in Cologne who had sent German students to the UK as part of the EU-sponsored Erasmus exchange programme. As a result, F4P were able to offer an opportunity for young German students to take part in this venture. What follows is an account of the Maagan project through the eyes of one German coach whose family, although not Jewish, themselves had experienced political upheaval after the Polish and German borders had been moved during the middle part of the last century. The information comes from a series of transcribed interviews that were carried out with him during and after the 2005 project.

As was the case with the English coaches involved in the project, the motivation was essentially intrinsic for the German coach and an oppor-tunity for him to gain professional training as well learn about the conflict that had existed since the creation of the state of Israel. This was exemplified during one of the pre-project interviews in which he commented on the aims of Football for Peace:

> Football for peace has the goal of bringing together Jewish and Arab kids and with the help of soccer, their collaboration and team work can be developed. Israel is well known for the degree of its conflict. It's one of the biggest conflicts in the world. To make a contribution, to see how the kids are, to see how the social structure is, to just play soccer with them and whether its different either in Germany or England, that was compelling for me.

As a German coach working in Israel the dynamics of the coaching team were unique compared to the profiles of other project staff and added a slightly different dimension. This was also accentuated by the historical context of Israel and the post 1947 agreement that saw many Jewish people return to their spiritual homes after the holocaust. This was a topic that the German coach had thought about and paid particular attention to, as high-lighted in his comments:

> As a German, teaching Jewish children about peace could be challenging but there is so much between our generation and the holocaust that we only know it from history books and not from our

own experiences. It's a distant view. Nevertheless, when you arrive at the airport and when you see these people, it makes a difference. You think about what happened in the past and what impact that had on so many families. You realise that here live many people and families that would have a completely different life at a different place if the incident didn't happen. All that creates a certain feeling of responsibility. It's difficult to describe. It's a feeling like it's good what we're doing especially with my German background, I'm extra dedicated and active to make a contribution.

One particular theme that emerged from the interviews with the German coach was his perceptions of the influence of parents and adults on the children and how they affected the children's views of each other. This had a significant impact on how the children responded to one another in the context of the mixed coaching groups they were in and presented a number of challenges in terms of implementing the core values and principles associated with the project as highlighted in the comments below:

Generally, I have to say that the kids are pretty influenced by their parents, even though I trained several teams in Germany where the parents interfered quite a lot too. But here the interference is special since it's the parents who fight in this conflict and they carry on this dispute to their children. So the interference of the parents has major consequences and the kids are very affected.

However, the project had provided the opportunity for the team of coaches to educate the parents through the children and provide a particular context for discussion between them, as the German coach related:

When I was invited for dinner one night I realised that this had a strong impact on the parents as well because after the training days the kids bring this home. They tell what they have experienced. These experiences have influenced them and they pass it on to their parents. So, in a way it educates the parents too. It's not just about the twelve kids in my group either.... It affects the whole family.

The continued influence of parents and significant others on the attitudes of children was potentially an issue that could affect the relationships within the groups and with the group leader. Learning about the depth of division and potential antagonism between Arabs and Jews from previous projects, however, helped to prepare the coaching staff in advance and, by focusing on the core themes and values of the project, the German coach was able to demonstrate how the principle of neutrality could be applied. For example, F4P is a politics-free zone and those who participate in F4P leave their political views and ideological positions outside even though the political tension and divide within their communities is very significant. In the context of the coaching that took place this was exemplified by the following account:

> Their older siblings, their parents, their friends are certainly emotionally affected by the situation in Israel and carry this forward to the kids. When you drive through Israel, you realise it's emotionally loaded. There are these strips in different colours that are attached to the cars. Orange means disengagement and blue, I think is the opposite. It splits the land into two camps. I didn't have the feeling that this played a role in my group but that's because we don't talk about it. It's not a matter for the project.

During the first morning of the first day of the project, the UK and Israeli coaches were introduced and spent some time discussing the day-by-day project plans. The first three days were to be spent taking the children through a basic soccer skills coaching programme. On the fourth day the children would be re-mixed into teams according to ability as well as religious affiliation/ethnicity. This was to ensure that teams would be evenly matched on the day of the tournament. The rest of the fourth day was spent engaging the groups with a series of team-building games and activities. In this respect, the community-relations dimension of the programme would be best served by subliminally emphasising the team-building process. This was to be supplemented by a series of recreational activities organised by local volunteers that would take place alongside the football programme as the different age groups were rotated. The final day consisted of a six-a-side tournament or festival of football. What follows is an account of the project as it unfolded.

As the children arrived on the first day there were understandable anxieties amongst them which the German coach reflected upon in his initial observations and how the themes and core values within the curriculum such as trust had helped him in to address the issues of group dynamics:

> I could clearly see that the kids didn't know each other very well. They didn't interact freely and they were a little tense. They didn't know each other's names. The behaviour of the kids was very typical. They were very distant in the beginning. They didn't talk to each other but I primarily picked exercises that strengthen trust so that the kids get to know each other and each other's names such as ice-breaker games with and without a ball. I built in these ice-breakers to develop a good basis for a good team.

After the first day it was very evident that the challenges of bringing children together from different cultural settings is not necessarily a straight-forward task and the individual coach has to work very hard in breaking down barriers. This was described in one of the interviews following the first day of coaching:

> Every year you get twelve kids and then you start. You see and feel that the kids don't know each other, that they come from different communities and that they're not one team. You have some individuals who you start to do some exercises with but they are neither motivated nor mobilized. It's just a strange mix for them and you have to start from zero. You don't know their characters and they don't know who they have in front of them. So it's a new situation for everyone. It's a new feeling. It's an exciting feeling. How will it be? What are the kids like?

In this respect, his previous experiences of other projects had helped in preparing for the uncertainties the coach had explained even though it still required careful thought, management and organisation:

> Since I know what a difference the first day makes, I think I am able to make a good team out of such a wild mix which makes me more confident but there is always uncertainty because the children are so different. You see the Arab kids on one side talking to each other, sticking together. Just next to them is the Jewish faction with the translators. So you see two camps that we have to bring together. But in the beginning they still stand there separately. Each time it's a big challenge and uncertainty mixed with fear of whether it's going to work out.

As the project evolved there were clearly noticeable improvements between the children and their interaction with each other but the German coach was keen to emphasise the importance of developing each of the core values as opposed to football skills and techniques. With respect to the children's own responsibility to each other the coach's approach was to remain peripheral, as shown in the following extract:

> Concerning my behaviour, I decided not to intervene, not to make decisions or direct but to leave it up to the kids. Everybody has their own style, of course, but generally we're required to step back. In other words, we arrange situations for the kids in which they interact and play but in which they also meet problems. We, as coaches do not intervene and solve the problem but we step back and observe.

This approach enabled the German coach to reinforce the notion of taking responsibility for individual actions but also to develop a sense of fairness. Examples of this are highlighted below:

> When the ball goes off and it's not clear whose throw-in it is, they immediately look to us. They see us as referees and expect us to make the decision with fouls or something. But I shake my head and suggest that they to find out themselves whose throw it is. It is difficult to set up, just to step back and observe and let the kids arrange things themselves. It arranges itself and eventually they accept each other's opinions and they find their own rules.

The emphasis on teaching core values was further explained with regard to the curriculum and how instilling positive behaviours in children was the main intention in preparing them for the tournament at the end of the week:

> The basic idea is to teach the fundamentals of soccer — ball familiarity, passing and receiving, dribbling, and finally attacking to shoot goals. Those are the four main columns. They function to communicate the four main goals such as trust, equity, responsibility and neutrality, not soccer skills. That means that I do exercises that have something to do with passing and receiving but at the same time they're used to for the kids to learn positive interaction with each other. So for me it's not important that someone receives the ball properly but I consider it a medium, an intermediary for this value. For me it is important how they deal with it when someone plays a bad pass for example. Is someone screaming at the other for screwing up the pass or do they just get the ball and continue?

Further discussion with the German coach revealed the extent to which the children began to interact more openly and how he developed cohesiveness within the group:

> Well, like I said, Sunday (the first day) was just to get to know each other, shake each other's hand and get in touch, but I didn't get the feeling that we were twelve friends that interact great with each other. One day later, only one day, I recognised a lot of signs of improvements in the kids' behaviour. One, they interacted a lot more and were relaxed and two, many of them already knew each other's names. I attach great importance to that they call each other's names very often. We also had the name tags for those who didn't know all the names yet. Me, too, by the way. I had to memorise the name list, however, and have to take a glance at their name tags. So by day two there is a lot of relief.

Towards the end of the training week there were some notable differences in the children's behaviour that were considered to be positive outcomes of the experiences they had received. This was particularly noticeable during the small-sided games that were often a highlight for the children and usually took place at the end of a session. The German coach was able to recount certain teachable moments in this respect:

> During the soccer games I watched how the opponents shot the ball out of play. A player from the other team ran after the ball and brought it back to his opponent who then took a throw in once he was back in play even though I didn't suggest it. This would have been uncommon early on. I try not to influence them by talking but I try to communicate what this is about. Also, I could observe how problems were solved very quickly — fouls for example. When the ball is kicked off, is it a corner or a goal kick? Whose throw is it? To begin with they'd look at me and because I just shrugged my shoulders and said 'I don't know', 'it's up to you', they solved this internally. It went pretty quick then, without any fighting. This impressed me. I found it a big improvement.

At the end of the four-day programme it was apparent that the group with whom the German coach had worked closely had begun to develop a sense of group identity particularly when associated with their given team name, Fulham, an English Premiership club. The coach had remarked on how well the team had worked together but was also keen to retain the core principles of the project as the final festival of football approached:

> I found the last training day the best one and the most fun. The kids were really motivated. We're one day before the tournament. After three days we have grown together pretty well and everything is great so far even though we have had a few problems. I am very satisfied with the kids and I'm confident that they will take what they have learned during the last three days into the tournament tomorrow. We have a few good players in the team, but it's not important who will win and I told them that. I hope they will behave in the way we agreed upon and I have really tried to teach them that. Winning is not supposed to be at the cost of fair play. If you lose, it happens. The question is how do you deal with it then? That will be the interesting part.

As in the previous year, the final tournament day was held in one central location, this time in the Arab town of Um al Fahem (a predominantly Moslem town), one of the project's partner communities and situated on the border with the Palestinian authority. The finals were to be held at the 'Peace Stadium' in the Arab town and involved over one thousand children from each of the individual project sites. Prior to the start of the tournament the German coach highlighted some of his initial apprehensions and referred to some anxieties with respect to the anticipated outcomes of the day.

> I find the situation here absolutely exciting. You have to imagine that the last four days we worked in a small group where you could achieve more and exert influence on the kids. Here, with so many kids in one place, there is a risk that what we have emphasised over the last four days will be totally ignored. I'm afraid that they may withdraw from that because they may let themselves get carried away by the wave that they must get into the finals or win the tournament.

After two draws and two victories 'Team Fulham' had qualified for the quarter finals. The manner in which the team had achieved this was particularly gratifying for the German coach:

> The team grew together. You saw how they celebrated and how they played together. They fought for each victory in a positive way. I don't mind if they want to win. It's a game, afterall, which is supposed to be won. But the way they acted and played was great.

Incredibly, the team had progressed beyond the quarter final and semi final stage and were due to play in the final of the younger boy's competition. This was achieved in spite of the fact that their opponents were technically superior.

> Our team was definitely not better. The players were not better than the opponents' players. In this respect, these were victories that lead back to community and team spirit. They performed as one team, they fought cohesively, they fought for every square inch of the ground, and they did this in a fair manner. And that's why they are in the finals now.

Having reached the final of the tournament 'Team Fulham' prepared to take on their opponents with an air of confidence in themselves and each other. Against all odds they scored the only goal of the game and pulled off an incredible victory. The German coach remained convinced that this had been achieved not so much through football skills but by taking responsibility for each other:

> As so often with kids, and especially, here, they are not used to making their own decisions and take responsibility for themselves or for others. Very often they are ... commanded by adults. They're being told what to do. You can see this in the treatment of one another on the pitch. Every time there is a decision to be made they look to the adults, to the referee, or to me to clarify the issue. From the beginning I told them that they deal with it themselves.... That they talk and they clarify the issues. Eventually it worked out great. At the end we had to pick one Jewish and one Arab kid from the team to pick up the trophy at the ceremony. I told them to decide and eventually they picked the player who scored the most goals and the goalkeeper. Responsibility is one of the main goals.

The level of commitment amongst the team had resulted in tournament victory despite their being less proficient in term of skills and techniques.

The achievement had emphasised the potential that team building in this context could have upon children from completely disparate backgrounds:

> I personally found it phenomenal that we won. I have never experienced anything like this. The fact is that there were nearly one thousand children and that makes it very special as the chance to win the tournament is very small especially as there were much better teams than us. We won against teams that were not as organised. In our team the substitutes were so excited about their goals they would run on the pitch and hug each other.... So such closeness was their strength and this is why we won the tournament. The team grew together and had a great team spirit and this why it is such a great accomplishment.

Leaders perspectives

Overall, the project at Maagan was a great success and involved nearly one hundred children. Each of the UK coaches worked with ten to twelve children aged between nine and thirteen years of age for two hours at a time. The withdrawal of facilities from the municipal council of El Battouf meant that a sub standard and potentially hazardous playing area in the community was not an adequate alternative and that project would remain in the Jewish area of Maagan. One of the Arab partners had explained that essential maintenance work was being carried out on the stadium facility and that the Mayor of El Battouf would not sanction any delay to the proposed work. As an alternative to this particular facility it was suggested that a concrete basketball type facility could be offered. Having considered the possible health and safety issues involved in having children playing football on this type of surface it was decided to continue the project at Maagan, which had proved to be a suitable facility for all concerned.

Other issues arose related to translation. The lack of Jewish and Arabic translators for each of the groups made the coaching particularly challenging but in most cases the UK team were able to adapt and cope with the situation. However, with a relatively inexperienced team of UK coaches the lack of two translators per group made the coaching very demanding, particularly for one UK coach who was unable to sustain any teaching quality and showed little or no understanding of the principles outlined within the coaching manual or during the training sessions provided both in the UK and Israel. This has very clear implications for future recruitment and the criteria upon which selection is based as well as the UK partner institutions that we choose to work with in future. This may involve more formalised recruitment and selection procedures in order to ensure both commitment and coaching expertise.

In some cases the translators that were provided were young members of the community with little or no experience of coaching whilst the more experienced translators had limited subject knowledge with respect to football and the core themes of the project. However, all communities were generally well organised and committed to the project and carried out their responsibilities well. Apart from the lack of a pitch in El Battouf, facilities were good overall and refreshments were provided to children and staff. Off-pitch activities were provided for the children in the form of swimming and orienteering and proved to be both popular and successful. In respect to the orienteering activities, children were provided a highly organised event whereby one child from each of the communities worked in groups of three in solving particular navigational problems.

The enthusiasm and motivation of the children was very apparent throughout the week and despite some initial anxieties amongst a few children on the first day they worked consistently hard and bonded well as a group. The relationship between the community leaders was also very positive and I spoke with them regularly about their thoughts and opinions about the project which were very positive. This was very evident on the final day when the children competed in the mixed teams that they had trained with throughout the first four days. There was a high level of commitment to the aims of the project amongst the community leaders reflected in their enthusiasm and the numbers of children provided. They regularly spoke of building cultural bridges as opposed to playing football. The physical distance between the communities was highlighted as a potential problem for future projects and it was suggested that clusters of communities within fifteen minutes of each other would be far better in terms of travelling times and the expense of hiring coach transportation.

Conclusion

In simplistic terms the children had an enormous amount of fun, learnt a bit of football, made new friends, were given opportunities to work with other children from different communities, and started to begin to view 'the other' in different ways. On reflection, it was clear that a focused approach to the teaching of desirable human qualities through the medium of football could be achieved and group cohesion could be developed. The fact that team Fulham, under the guidance of their German coach, accomplished overall success in the final tournament is incidental but is nonetheless testament to potential impact and outcomes that the F4P curriculum could have upon such a disparate group of children. They did not win because they were the best footballers, but because they were the best team. Whilst their technical ability was no more than average, their commitment towards each other and their willingness to work as a unit had enabled them to progress through a series of competitive games and ultimately win the final. Certainly, the views of their German coach would support such an assessment of their performance in that they beat stronger opposition, played as a team and took responsibility for individual roles that were assigned to them. Collectively, this had enabled them to build relationships with each other, gain a sense of achievement and develop positive attitudes towards themselves and other children within their team. Moreover, it had assisted in helping these children develop social skills involving co-operation and collaboration, responsibility, personal commitment, loyalty and teamwork, as well as enabling them to consider the social importance of physical activity and sport.

Overall, the Football 4 Peace programme had provided these particular children an experience they could share with their respective friends and families within their own communities and an insight into the positive effects that well-managed programmes such as this could have on their overall perspectives with regards to each other. In a small, but nonetheless significant way, the cascading effect of these experiences upon the extended families of both Jewish and Arab children may have contributed towards an understanding of the significance of these types of activities from their own and other cultures, and subsequently lead them to recognise how activities and public performance give a sense of cultural identity, and consider how sport can transcend cultural boundaries. Ultimately this can develop positive behaviours and attitudes that transfer beyond the football pitch and encourage team bonding and respect amongst young people who may share experiences and empathy for one another and enable them to become responsible citizens of their own communities.

Chapter 7

ON SHIFTING SANDS: THE COMPLEXITIES OF WOMEN'S AND GIRLS' INVOLVEMENT IN FOOTBALL FOR PEACE

Jayne Caudwell

Introduction

This chapter explores some experiences of women coaches from UK Univer-sities working on the Football for Peace (F4P) project in 2005. The chapter provides a particular account of gender relations, football and cultural sensi-bilities. I write from a feminist perspective and as a white academic about a football project in Israel. The context is undeniably complicated given Israel's political and religious backdrop and the socially constructed config-urations of gender relations that have emerged as a result.

In many ways it is the blatant exclusion of girl players from the project's showcase grand finale which provides the fulcrum for critical discussion of gender relations. This incident contrasted with my experience as project leader in the communities of I'blin and Misgav which had been quite inclusive, albeit within a broader context of patriarchal domination. Necessarily the discussions on gender relations aim to make visible the intricacies and complexities that are characteristic of women's and girls' involvement in F4P.

The chapter introduces sports feminist work on sportswomen's and girls' experiences of Moslem culture and politics. Literature evidences the sporting experiences of Moslem women and girls living in the UK (Kay, 2005; Lowrie and Kay, 2005; Zaman, 1997), and the experiences of women and girls living in countries that are predominantly Moslem, for example, Egypt (Balboul, 2000; Walseth and Fasting, 2003) and North Africa (Hargreaves,

2000). The chapter then documents gendered experiences of some women coaches in relation to F4P and the exclusion of girl players from the final day, and finishes with critical reflection on the ways the spatiality of sexuality informs gender relations.

The context

Women's involvement in F4P has gradually increased since the first project in I'blin in 2001. In 2002, the Jewish communities of Misgav and Tivon joined I'blin, eight coaches and two staff leaders delivered values-based football to 150 children, and this figure included 20 girls (Sugden, 2005). An all-girl project in Tiberias, staffed by women coaches and translators, was introduced in 2004 and in 2005 the girls' project was extended to include the communities of Sakhnin and Akko, as well as Tiberias. With increased community involvement and increased participation by girls, women's involvement in coaching and leadership also increased. In 2005, the girls' project was headed by a woman and consisted of 2–3 women coaches. In addition, I led a team of 4 coaches, which included one woman. Out of the six remaining projects, there was a woman coach in all but one of the communities. In total, of the coaching/leading group of 40, 11 were women, just over a quarter of the staff.

The communities of I'blin and Misgav have a four-year history of engagement with F4P. Representatives from each community appeared very committed to ideas surrounding values-based football. The level of commitment meant that the two key workers, both men, one from each community, were well-organised with good communication links. As with other projects, the first day involved integrating players, boys in this case, into mixed-community teams. Each project had the potential to deliver to 100 children; 50 from each community and split between two age groups (10–11 year olds and 12–13 year olds).

The coaching team consisted of myself and four recently qualified Physical Education teachers, one woman and three men. As a group of five we stayed at a local Kibbutz. We were collected every day by a representative from Misgav, taken for lunch and then on to I'blin to the pitch, which was grassed, in good condition and well maintained. It was situated on flat land skirting I'blin and was surrounded by corrugated iron walling. About 50 local children, most of them walking, came down from the densely-housed town perched on the hillside. By way of recognising and celebrating I'blin and the people of I'blin, Arabic children and translators often told us that it had two churches and two Mosques, which were visible from the pitch. In fact the Arab town is 50% Moslem and 50% Christian and the two groups tend to live in separate neighbourhoods and mix in separate social circles. This reflects a more widespread and less well known sectarian geography in the region.

The four translators from I'blin were all Moslem and included a young woman and a young man, both under twenty, and two older men. At the end of each of our four days coaching we were invited into their homes to eat. We met their families and sat and ate traditional Arabic food with them. We spent Saturday, Sunday, Monday and Wednesday evenings in I'blin and became familiar with some of the history and culture of the community. In fact, one evening we were taken to the local mosque and told about aspects of Islam.

Misgav is a widespread municipality and the boys who came from from there had to travel, by bus, from their outlying residences and dispersed communities. On the first day, it was apparent that only 35 Jewish boys had attended. At the end of the first session the I'blin and Misgav representatives approached me with an idea they had obviously already discussed. The suggestion was to include girls from I'blin which had a thriving girls soccer programme. After further discussion, we all agreed that this would be both possible and desirable. The next morning, a number of girls aged about 10–12 arrived with the older age group. This meant that each coach added 2–3 new players to their previously all-boy groups.

Translators from Misgav included one young woman and two young men, all under twenty years old, and an older man. We spent our lunch-times with them, sometimes in their homes and twice at local eating places, both of which were Arab-owned kebab-style restaurants. On our final evening in I'blin, the three younger Jewish translators were invited to join us and three of the Arabic translators for the evening meal in the home of one of the Arabic translators. On this occasion, the young translators from I'blin and Misgav and coaches from University of Brighton spent an evening together.

During our time on the project it was apparent that links between the two communities extended beyond the children's mixed football teams. Not only were the children, boys and girls, playing alongside each other, the translators and organisers were also forging relationships. In other words, there were several layers of integration, which extended beyond the time on, and space of, the football pitch. These relationships are significant given that the two communities co-exist in a relatively small geographical area, but are segregated. It became apparent during the 6 days of F4P that local community relations were very good.

Above is a sketch of the context for discussions that follow. In addition to the research context, it is also important to make visible the social location of the researcher. For me, such transparency demonstrates that claims to knowledge are at best, incomplete and that processes of knowledge production are political. I entered the research context as a football player and coach, white, middle-class, 'Western-feminist', and as an 'unmarried', 'childless', 'older' woman. Such social and cultural locations impact on my experiences of F4P in Israel, and, how I interpret these experiences.

Discussions presented in this chapter rely on qualitative research material, namely observation and conversation — what happened and what was said. In this way everyday practices in specific football settings are used to help explain how women's experiences of the game are socially constructed. During the ten day visit, July 7th–17th, 2005, a research diary was kept and it is these field notes that underpin analysis. The field diary was used to record conversation and observation.

Research findings are presented, in sections headed 'gendered experiences' and 'feminist reflection'. Qualitative research methodology is used to bring to the fore auto/biography (Bruce, 1998). The account is based on the voices of several women involved in the project, as well as my own. I have selected particular comments from the research diary field notes to highlight everyday practices. Discussion centres on gendered aspects of working in football in a specific social, cultural and political setting.

A brief literature review

At the time of writing, any mention of football and Israel usually elicits comment about the Jewish-Arab [men's] side from Sakhnin playing Newcastle United in the Uefa Cup (Blackburn, 2004) and the fact that Israel and England are in the same group for 2008 (men's) European Nations Cup. Importantly, academic commentary illustrates how football in Israel is embedded in a complex arrangement of ethnic relations. For example, Sorek (2005) provides a detailed account of the historical and political relevance of the team from Sakhnin. He demonstrates the team's significance, both locally and globally, and centres analysis on the diversity of ethnicity evident at the football club. Similar accounts (Ben-Porat, 2001; Sorek, 2003) further explore the unique place of football in Israeli society.

As with literature on football in other countries the game usually remains unmarked as "men's". Given this starting point, women's participation becomes "women's football". In both popular cultural practice and academic analysis it is men who are legitimised, through language and inference, as footballers. Women become "women footballers". Such naming has multiple effects. It can function to propel a liberal policy agenda of increased access and opportunity. In most countries, "women footballers" are a minority. Sugden (2005), using statistics from a 2000 survey (Israel Women's Network, 2002), describes the situation in Israel: "Worst of all was the gendered imbalance in football where, out of a total of 32,000 registered players, only 1,000 were female, barely more than 3%" (p. 3). Once identified as a minority group, "women footballers" can then be targeted with resources to help increase participation. However, a liberal agenda forgets women's struggles based on social and cultural practices that de-value their involvement. "Football" is implicitly understood as a men's activity. The label "women's football" reflects processes of 'othering'. In this way, naming impacts on ownership of and entitlement to the game. It becomes apparent that being in a minority is often synonymous with being marginalised. The coupling is a result of the operations of power. It is this inextricable relationship between minority status and processes of marginalisation that a liberal agenda can fail to recognise.

Feminist debates on naming sports and tensions surrounding a liberal approach to equality are not new (Hargreaves, 1994; Scraton and Flintoff, 2002). Inclusion in this chapter serves as a reminder and, inadvertently, casts a critical lens on F4P. Clearly, the dilemmas facing F4P and gender inequality are further complicated because of existing gender relations apparent in some Moslem communities in Israel.

Feminist researchers demonstrate the inequalities women and girls can experience in countries that are predominantly Moslem (Balbour, 2000; Hargreaves, 2000; Walseth and Fasting, 2003) and countries that are not (Lowrie and Kay, 2005; and Kay, 2005; Zaman, 1997). Balboul (2000) makes the point, one which is made by most writers, that "Islam is not opposed to women's participation in physical activities, on the contrary, it favours such activities" (p. 168). Given this premise, research tends to explore experiences of participation. Interestingly, reference to the 'veil' is often used to denote the restrictions facing Moslem women. For example, a recent article in the *Guardian* (7 November, 2005) epitomises this — *The Veil is Slowly Lifting for Moslem Women Athletes* (Bee, 2005). In many ways, reference to the 'veil' draws attention to the body, modesty and dress. However, it tends to be 'dress' that becomes the focus of concern. Importantly, Ali (1992, cited in Zaman, 1997: p. 51) argues that "the issue confronting Moslem women should not be reduced to 'dress'". Her insistence that debate must run deeper and be more extensive than mere 'dress' must remain a central aspect of sports feminism.

Hargreaves (2000) provides a detailed celebration of the achievements of Moslem women, in particular in Iran and Algeria, and generally on the international stages of sport. She cites evidence of women in Iran playing football and defiantly entering public arenas to watch men play: "Women's soccer is now allowed, the training of women coaches and referees began in early 1998, and a permanent women's section in major stadia have been set up" (p. 60). Similar acts of determination are evident in Egypt. Sahar El-Hawary, reputed for her work to establish indoor football, 11-a-side football, a football league and national team which attended the African Nations Cup in Nigeria in 1998, became "the first African Egyptian Arabic woman on the FIFA committee" (Hargreaves, 2000: p. 77). The focus on Moslem women's achievements shifts debate away from preoccupation with 'dress' and a concomitant 'problem-led' approach. Instead, explorations of diversity of Moslem culture and influences of Islam operate to dispel the myth of a unitary category: 'Moslem women'. As Hargreaves identifies, it is impossible to universalise Moslem women's experiences of sport.

Identifying Moslem women's different experiences of sport has provoked research into individual interpretation of Islam (Walseth and Fasting, 2003) and exploration of local context such as family (Kay, 2005). Walseth and Fasting (2003) research the relationship between Islam and physical activity in Egypt. They present findings on the ways young women, informed by Islam, are active. Kay's (2005) research with girls aged between 13–18 years, from a town in the Midland region of England centres upon the influence of family relationships and the "spatial scope of the girls' activities" (p. 109). Home emerged as the space they spent most time. Although their lives were home-based they were still able to take part in the Widening Access Through Sport (WATS) project under investigation.

From existing literature we are able to gain insights into conditions facing Moslem girls and women in their quest to take part in sport and physical activity. Further work is needed that considers the many ways Moslem women successfully take part in sport. Despite major hostility and protest Moslem women have 'played on'. For example, Malika Chandoo captained the Britain's Moslem women's football team in the 2001 Moslem Women's Games; Rakia Al-Gassra ran in the 100metres at Athens 2004; the Bangladesh Football Federation (BFF) helped a 20-member Under-17 team prepare and participate in the Asian Football Confederation Women's Football Championship in South Korea, 2005; and Sania Mirza continues to play tennis on the international women's circuit.

Currently, we know little about white women's experiences of working in sport related projects and initiatives embedded in Moslem communities and Moslem culture. F4P is such a project; it offers a new context for exploring Moslem sensibilities, gender and sport. An inclusion of white women's experiences is important for three reasons. Firstly, it resists the tendency to compare participation levels between 'Western' women and Moslem women. Secondly, it seeks to complicate our understanding of liberal agendas to promote equality/inequality. Finally, experiences of the white women involved in the project highlight the significance of space and spatiality to an understanding of sport and Moslem culture.

Gendered experiences

As is related in earlier chapters of this volume, we left the UK for Tel Aviv on July 7, the evening of the 2005 London bombings. Four men had killed 52 people and themselves as they travelled on public transport. I heard the news on the radio and imagined the carnage as it would appear on television scenes. Images of death and destruction running through my mind's eye merged with already formed images of the media's coverage of the West's 'war against terror'. In my shock, pictures of the conflict in Israel joined with these images and the figures in my mind almost always were of men — masses of men fighting and filling public spaces. Such an over-simplification is obviously problematic; nevertheless, it was an emotive way to understand the brutality of events.

During our first few days in Israel it became obvious that the spaces we occupied as a group were predominantly male spaces. Despite numbers of women coaches involved in the project, it was apparent that unfamiliar gender relations prevailed. Five of the eleven women coaches worked in coaching teams as the only female, delivering to all-boy groups. Such a situation can cause a sense of isolation especially if their presence is undermined. Practices of marginalisation can be slight. A few women talked about how some boys refused to cooperate and/or engage. These boys might not have been coached by a woman before. Their understanding of [men's] football legitimises men's involvement, even if these men do not play or coach as well as women. Given these assumptions, a few women coaches were faced with a situation where they had to prove themselves. In this way, battles for equality resided with individual women and became wearisome.

One of the women talked about her feelings of being excluded during off-pitch liaisons with local organisers who in all cases were men. Formal greetings and introductions between men are well rehearsed in public. The inclusion of women into such rituals, especially among men who are reluctant to shake hands with women, can dislocate proceedings. The woman who spoke to me about her experiences was astounded by the blatant denial to make acquaintances. The [non]gesture then became familiar to her as it happened a few more times. I asked her what her male colleagues thought about it. She believed that they did not notice and were therefore unable to comment.

The four women coaches working together on the girls-only project also experienced gendered responses to their presence. They were housed in the local Arab community. Unlike most of the other projects, the all-girls project suffered from a lack of local preparation, organisation and equipment. It was one of a couple of projects that required further work once we arrived in Israel. The coaching team adjusted to poor facilities, difficult working conditions and restrictions on their evening activities. Once in the local community their conspicuous presence, as a group of young women, meant a certain amount of chaperoning. In effect they did not feel they had the freedom to roam the locality. The gendering of public spaces has been a key issue for 'Western' feminist geographers for some time (Duncan, 1996; Massey, 1994). The tradition of men's presence in workplaces, sports arenas, and city streets in many societies has effectively marked 'public' spaces as male. Despite women's increasing visibility in public, in some communities the streets remain contested terrain. For the women coaches this was the situation they faced for four out of six evenings/nights. Eventually they requested a move and were given new residences.

At times, being a white woman in Moslem communities and homes disturbs the binary gendering of relations between men and women. In *The Book Seller of Kabul*, Asne Seierstad (a white female journalist) provides a compelling account of gender relations in Afghanistan in late 2001 and early 2002. She lives for a time within the domestic arrangement of a family, headed by Sultan, the book's protagonist. He rules over his family's affairs, and takes a second wife, a teenage bride, when he is in his early 50s. Seierstad writes of how her whiteness gave her certain privileges Afghani women are denied:

> I imagine they regard me as some sort of 'bi-gendered' creature. As a westerner I could mingle with both men and women... there was no obstacle to my being a woman, in a man's world. When the feasts were split, men and women in separate rooms, I was the only one able to circulate freely between groups. (p. 5/6)

Sierstad illustrates the impossibilities of writing about women's experiences as unified. She also highlights how white women can take up positions of power when living in cultures that are inherently sexist towards indigenous women.

Being a woman football coach in Israel, working in predominantly Arab communities, raised similar gender issues. Obviously tensions here do not replicate the situation in Afghanistan. However, because some of the women coaches entered the homes of Moslem Arab families, traditions surrounding meal times emphasised gender inequalities:

> We were told to hurry up by one of the men because the other man's wife had been cooking all day. When we got there we didn't even see his wife, she stayed in the kitchen. And when one of the boys [UK coach] tried to help clear up he got told to leave it and sit down.

For some coaches whose hosts welcomed them into their homes this situation became familiar. For the women coaches their position as privileged guest at the table, an eating table that in some cases had a head and provided a symbolic representation of father-son male hierarchy, became an uncomfortable affair of which they were conscious. The confining of the women of the house to domestic duties and in some cases the literal space of the kitchen reflects gendered rituals surrounding meal times. It also alludes to the public-private split feminists have been keen to politicise (Oakley, 1972; Walby, 1990). It seemed that men occupied public space, for example football, and women the private spaces of domesticity. These practices were not only unusual for the UK women coaches but also impacted on male coaches who were unfamiliar with such tradition, as is highlighted above.

Returning to the all-girl project and coaching team, the biggest gender inequality they experienced was exclusion from the finals day. On the evening of day four it became common knowledge that girls had been denied access to the tournament. The event, planned to be held in Um al Fahem, a stronghold for pro-Islamic political organisations, was drawn to the attention of the Mayors Office after residents complained about women training/playing at the facility during the training day. It is difficult to establish exact reasons for the exclusion, but stories surrounding women performing sport in front of men, and women immodestly displaying their bodies, gained currency. Within Islamic law such behaviour is prohibited. In fact, it transpired that there was some confusion over the age of par-ticipants because it was women coaches that had been seen, but this was enough for the Mayor's Office to issue what amounted to a *fatwa* [legal pronouncement] banning any further female participation. If this was not agreed then permission to hold the finals tournament at the town's Stadium of Peace would be withdrawn. The details of this are made clear in the following *fatwa* issued by Sheikh Faysal Mawlawi, deputy Chairman of European Council for Fatwa and Research:

> The requirements to be met for a Muslim woman to practice sport relate, at all scales, to her duty to cover the *awrah* [parts of the body that are not supposed to be exposed to others; vis-à-vis women, her *awrah* is from the navel to the knee; as for men, it is all of her body except the hands, feet and face]. Thus, if there is a sport that a woman can practice while adhering to this requirement, then it is permissible for her so long as all other religious requirements are fulfilled ...[in addition] They must not intermingle with men in any way that brings them physically close together and there should be no kind of photographing or television that may broadcast these scenes. (Islam on Line, 2004)

For me, exclusion was infuriating given that the I'blin-Misgav project, with support from local organisers, had successfully integrated Jewish and Arab boys and Arab girls. The I'blin girls appeared to come to terms with the news that they could not play in the teams they had been with for three days. Their response was to sit together and form their own team. The team went to the girls' tournament and played a few games together before being split up on the basis that it was an all-Arabic team. This proved another disappointment for them.

A further consequence of exclusion was that the coaching team for the girls-only project became responsible for the new, separate girls' event. They had a day to prepare; this extra work-load came on top of a difficult week. During a preparatory meeting one male coach/leader volunteered to help with organisation. The girls' tournament ran relatively smoothly. I travelled to Um al Fahem, then with the girls from I'blin and their parents and supporters to a nearby Kibbutz for the girls' tournament. We travelled back to Um al Fahem to honour the winners, watch the firework grand finale and hear choruses of "all together now" — the project's unofficial anthem. The stadium where the boys had been playing was busy with spectators and officials, the pitches were properly marked and the atmosphere reflected that of a major sporting event. In comparison to this public display and celebration of boys' value-based football, the girls' tournament was the 'other'; it was less public and less prestigious.

In a quest by F4P organisers to denote girls' and women's marginal inclusion in the event one of the finals was refereed by a woman. In addition, the girls were given red t-shirts (provided by The (English) Football Association) to wear on their arrival. In the end and despite the exclusion, all the children, boys and girls, from eight projects were brought together.

The F4P project is founded on five principal values: equity, inclusion, respect, trust and responsibility, and neutrality. When applied to football as a way to build bridges between divided societies the values make sense. However, given experiences of gender inequality in 2005 the values dissolve. Undeniably, liberal agendas do give rise to successes, and in many ways F4P 2005 was a success. However, as previously mentioned, liberal approaches often forget structures and relations of power. For me, the final event and venue stretched the potential of F4P to a point of fracture. Unsurprisingly, it was the women and girls who experienced the full impact. I believe men involved in the project were also significantly affected and these shared experiences of disappointment can mobilise new ways to implement change. The challenge is to produce imaginative ways, within a liberal agenda, to ensure that girls as well as boys feel the impact of the values: equity, inclusion, respect, trust and responsibility, and neutrality.

Feminist reflection

Is there a nascent female liberation movement in the Middle East and North Africa similar to those in Western countries? For decades this kind of question has blocked and distorted analysis of the situation of Moslem women, keeping it at the level of senseless comparisons and unfounded conclusions. (Mernissi, 2003: p. 7)

Mernissi warns of the dangers of attempting to universalise women's exper-iences of gender. In her account she moves beyond Western feminist notions of gender relations and focuses inquiry on social arrangements of sexuality. Interestingly, while Western liberal feminist agendas for equality remain bound to the concept of gender, radical feminist and poststructuralist feminist contributions are more likely to imbricate *sexuality* and gender. For Mernissi, Moslem social order is founded on regulation of female sexuality and male-female relations. Despite her reluctance to make comparisons between the 'West' and Moslem Societies, she believes that "sexual inequality is the basis of both systems" (p. 8). For example, she compares the claims of Imam Ghazali and Freud. Both men have produced knowledge claims in relation to women's sexuality which have accepted as legitimate. The results are models of women's sexuality as active and/or passive:

> The irony is that Moslem and European theories come to the same conclusion: women are destructive to the social order — for Imam Ghazia because they are active, for Freud because they are not. (Mernissi, 2003: p. 44)

Mernissi further argues that because Islam positions women as active and therefore powerful and dangerous, "all sexual institutions (polygamy, repudiation, sexual segregation, etc.) can be perceived as a strategy for con-taining their power" (p. 19). The same is true of rituals of seclusion and sur-veillance. Processes of surveillance and seclusion function to divide Moslem society into two spheres:

> ... the universe of men (the *umma,* the world of religion and power) and the universe of women, the domestic world of sexuality and the family... The division is based on the physical separation of the *umma* (the public sphere) from the domestic universe. (Mernissi, 2003: p. 138)

Space is used territorially to regulate female sexuality and male-female relations. Surveillance and seclusion [of women] enable the strict alloca-tion of space for each sex. For Moslem societies that adopt such a regime, women's trespass into the *umma* is ritualised. However, there are no rituals to guide the presence of non-Moslem women. As Mernissi points out:

> There are no accepted patterns for interactions between unrelated
> men and women. Such interactions violate the spatial rules that are
> the pillars of the Moslem sexual order... Since the interaction of
> unrelated men and women is illicit, there are no rules governing
> it. (p. 137)

Difficulties experienced by the women coaches and the ultimate exclusion
of girls from the final event can be understood in relation to the spatiality
of sexuality. The rigorous marking of public space — *umma* — as male, in
Moslem culture, has a huge impact on participation in sport, especially given
the dominant view of sport, in 'Western' culture, that it is performed in
public arenas.

Spatiality of sexuality in Israel is interesting given that Jewish communities exist alongside Moslem and Christian communities and interpretations of religious law differ from one community to the next. Such
circumstance implies that public spaces and sporting spaces become a
mosaic of conventions, rituals and practices in relation to gender. By taking
account of these different public spaces it might be possible to tread
more carefully when attempting to achieve equity and integration for women
and girls.

Concluding comments

As Ali (1992, cited in Zaman, 1997) and Mernissi (2003) argue, little is
achieved from making comparisons between Moslem women's experience
and 'Western' women's experience. Not least because 'Western' experiences
are often positioned as the 'norm'. Their advocacy has important ramifi-
cations for liberal agendas of equality and implementation of values-based
sports initiatives.

Clearly, women and girls experience gender, sexuality, public space and
football in different ways compared to men and boys. This is the case in
'Western' societies as well as Moslem societies. Understanding the differences and nuances can help towards planning values-based sports projects.
Liberal agendas can and do promote egalitarianism if implemented with
insight and foresight, therefore, they are worth pursuing.

To reiterate, F4P 2005 had many successes and these are not to be
forgotten given current global tensions between the 'West' and some Moslem
cultures, and the situation now facing Israel in relation to an elected Hamas

political party in power in Palestine. Successes occurred at the local level and within community based projects. My lasting memories are of hot, sunshine-filled late afternoons, watching young people *playing* football together. Play was facilitated by talented and sensitive coaches who made the children laugh and run around happily while kicking a football. As the days went by the children began to hug each other, smile at each other, collect the ball for each other and help each other up, even argue over offering the opposition kick-off. Within the confines of the walled I'blin football pitch, the aims of F4P were achieved many times. In many ways there was no need to celebrate these achievements elsewhere since the successes belong to the communities of Misgav and I'blin.

References

Balboul, L. (2000) 'Sporting females in Egypt: Veiling or unveiling, an analysis of the debate', in S. Scraton and B. Watson (eds) *Sport, leisure identities and gendered spaces* (LSA Publication No. 67). Eastbourne: Leisure Studies Association.

Bee, P. (2005) 'The veil is slowly lifting for Moslem women athletes', *The Guardian,* 7th November, 2005.

Blackburn, N. (2004) 'A team of two halves', *The Times,* 16th September: p. 7.

Duncan, N. (1996) *Body space.* London: Routledge.

Gentleman, A. (2006) 'India's most wanted', *The Observer, OSM,* 5th February, pp. 54–61.

Hargreaves, J. (2000) *Heroines of sport. The politics of difference and identity.* London: Routledge.

Kay, T. (2005) 'The voice of the family: Influences on Moslem girls' responses to sport', in A. Flintoff, J. Long and K. Hylton (eds) *Youth, sport and active leisure: Theory, policy and participation* (LSA Publication No. 87). Eastbourne: Leisure Studies Association, pp. 91–114.

Lowrey, J. and Kay, T. (2005) 'Doing sport, doing inclusion: An analysis of provider and participant perceptions of targeted sport provision for young Moslems', in A. Flintoff, J. Long and K. Hylton (eds) *Youth, sport and active leisure: Theory, policy and participation* (LSA Publication No. 87). Eastbourne: Leisure Studies Association, pp. 73–90.

Massey, D. (1994) *Space, place and gender.* Cambridge: Polity Press.

Mernissi, F. (2003) *Beyond the veil. Male-female dynamics in Moslem society.* London: Saqi Books

Oakley, A. (1972) *Sex, gender and society.* Hants: Gower Press.

Seierstad, A. (2002) *The bookseller of Kabul.* London: Virago Press.

Sorek, T. (2005) 'Between football and martydom: The bi-focal localism of an Arab-Palestinian town in Israel', *The British Journal of Sociology* Vol. 56, No. 4, pp. 635–661.

Sugden, J. (2005) *The challenge of using a values-based approach to coaching sport and community relations in multi-cultural settings. The case of Football for Peace (F4P) in Israel.* Paper presented at the 3rd World Congress of Sociology of Sport. Buenos Aires, Argentina: November 30–December 3, 2005.

Walby, S. (1990) *Theorising patriarchy.* Cambridge: Polity Press

Walseth, K. and Fasting, K. (2003) 'Islam's view on physical activity and sport: Egyptian women interpreting Islam', *International Review for the Sociology of Sport,* Vol. 38, No. 1: pp. 45–60.

Zaman, H. (1997) 'Islam, well-being and physical activity: Perceptions of Moslem young women', in G. Clarke and B. Humberstone (eds) *Researching women and sport.* London: Macmillan, pp. 50–67.

Chapter 8

FOOTBALL FOR PEACE: A STUDENT VOLUNTEER'S PERSPECTIVE

Chris Howarth

For many students, beginning university life brings the desire to seek out and discover new experiences, embrace challenges and attempt to realise one's potential. You enter into a new world of possibility, with many different paths open to follow. With such opportunity at your finger tips you feel energised to find out about yourself, and you feel compelled to offer what you can give and to find out about the world around you for yourself. I was determined to be true to this 'philosophy' throughout my university life. For me, this was certainly the case when the Football for Peace (F4P) project came to my attention.

As a result of volunteering for involvement in Football for Peace in 2002, during my first year of study at the University of Brighton, I was also able to be a member of the 2003 and 2004 F4P projects before I finished my three year course. With this experience behind me I was delighted to be given the chance to work on the 2005 project where I took on the role of sub-project leader. This four year involvement has meant I have been lucky enough to see the project grow and develop, with the F4P aims and values reaching more children and more communities. With its particular aims and objectives, I have witnessed the impact and increased significance of the project within numerous communities. I have also been able to reflect on my own personal growth and the ways in which my opinions and perceptions have been able to develop, fed by my own experiences rather than those portrayed in the media. For me F4P has been a constant voyage of discovery from the first time I began to learn about Israel, the first moments of nervous anticipation as the plane approached Tel Aviv airport in 2002, and to the final few days of the 2005 project. The landscape of the project has been ever changing and developing with new challenges and new experiences always presenting themselves. I have personally experienced and been witness to moments of elation, immense satisfaction, privilege and achievement, as well as disappointments, setbacks and difficulties all within both the general context of the project, and specifically in relation to the football coaching within the communities.

The following chapter provides an insight into my experiences on the Israel F4P project as a student volunteer. Much of its content will reflect upon recurrent themes and observations across four years of work for F4P. Included in this is my transition to project leader in 2005 and the additional challenges that confronted me. I was fortunate enough to be at the Univer- sity of Brighton as F4P was evolving from innovative ideas into strategic direction and action. Without a great deal of knowledge of the background or intentions of the project I was given the opportunity to run in the 2002 London Marathon and to raise sponsorship with the intention of financing F4P for its second year. With this opportunity I became physically and emo- tionally entwined with the project and developed a personal interest in its central philosophy and growth. It was clear from this early stage that my relative ignorance of the political and social backdrop of Israel was replicated in the other volunteer students. There were certainly more questions than answers on the precise nature of what we had let ourselves in for.

As a new student ready to embrace my new university career, I very quickly realised the Israel project suited me in many ways. It was undoubt- edly going to be a unique experience with new people, new environment, an unprecedented level of challenge, as well as opportunities to develop personally and to find out about myself. These were just some of the things I felt sure would characterise the project. After many conversations with my fellow student volunteers I soon discovered, that, like me, they viewed university as a place of opportunity and discovery and for us all the Israel project epitomised this positive outlook. In a sense, and without knowing it at the time, we shared a set of common values, a theme which would evolve to become the central theme of F4P in years to come.

As student volunteers preparing for the F4P project we became increasingly educated, through reading and listening, about the situation in Israel and about the specific aims, objectives and values of the project. For me the responsibility and commitment required as a volunteer on this project quickly became clear. This project is about encouraging and working towards peaceful co-existence and conflict resolution. Football, the global game, is simply the medium that brings together the Arab and Jewish communities, in the shape of their children, local coaches and parents. They, but more specifically their children, could understand the values that permeated the football experience and recognise how they could operate within their daily lives. Albeit small in scope, the significance of the project within a nation currently divided but working, albeit slowly, towards achieving peaceful co-existence should not be underestimated.

As coaches we are there to work to transmit and encourage these values through football and to be positive, enthusiastic role models. To add further challenge this task was to be undertaken within hot, unfamiliar conditions and communicating with the children predominantly through an interpreter. The process of adjusting to the demands of such an environment in one of the most divided societies in the world continues to intrigue and excite me. However, these positive emotions need to be separated from the negative feelings of fear and anxiety which have, at times, required rational thought and much soul searching. Not least during occasions when there is increased alert in the Middle East, or the London bombings in 2005 on the day of our departure to Israel, and the conflict with Hezbollah in Lebanon in 2006 which caused the project to be called off only moments before we boarded the plane for Tel Aviv.

I am no stranger to conflict. I am not referring to the conflict on a macro level, between two warring factions or the one that we are trying to do our bit to help resolve. My conflict as F4P approaches always seems to revolve around trying to resolve my own personal and emotional issues. On the one side is the nervous apprehension caused by media images of suicide bombings in a country under constant threat of terrorism and civil dispute. This is aligned with the interrogation of friends and relatives who, like me, have only been subjected to a very limited and probably distorted picture of Israel through the media. On the other side is my stated philosophy of seeing the world for myself, formulating my own standpoint based on experience and accepting challenges in a quest for knowledge and self fulfilment.

This emotional conflict is uncomfortable and must be resolved. It is clear that some prospective volunteers have previously resolved this dissonance by withdrawing from the project. Given the nature of the information presented to us on an almost daily basis and the pressure we all get from friends and relatives, this is completely understandable. For me the most proactive way of dealing with this problem has been the quest for a more rounded and balanced view of the social and political situation in Israel. During this period it quickly became evident to me that when Israel featured on the news it was to report some violent act of destruction born out of the conflict — another location, another suicide bomber, another series of casualties and the region being plunged further into religion-fuelled hatred and violence. I always made a conscious effort to remain objective in the face of news emerging from Israel. In reality BBC News 24 and related broadcasters can only be used as a starting point for researching a more accurate and enduring picture of Israel. I was keen to delve deeper into Israeli history and society. I took time to research the communities themselves, the geography of the Galilee region in Northern Israel which is the location for all of the F4P projects, and most importantly of all the demographics of the region we would be working in. Outcomes of my research went some way to resolving the dissonance that I felt in making the decision to be involved in the project. The picture that emerged was one of a much less volatile society and one which, surprisingly, is far more secular that I ever imagined.

The point of my pragmatic approach was to ascertain the extent of the work many ordinary people throughout Israel are doing to try and achieve peace. We do not hear the informed and constructive opinions and voices of local people and we cannot begin to picture the parts of the country that are not war torn, which is reality is the vast majority. Very soon after arriving in Israel it becomes apparent that it is a country that you have to experience if you want to gain an accurate, holistic understanding of what is a very complicated and, in many ways, unique country.

However, prior to my first visit to Israel I could not help but be influenced by the news features I was seeing and reading. I recall landing in Israel, in Tel Aviv, for the first time and just feeling a sense of unease and danger. I felt uncomfortable in the new environment and everything seemed to have an air of unpredictability. With time, experiences and ever improving knowledge of my surroundings, these feelings diminished and were replaced by a greater confidence and sense of security. I could view the country not through the eyes of the BBC or The Guardian, but through my own, and it was a much-improved sight. With every subsequent visit the conflict in my mind becomes easier to resolve as I carry vivid memories of friends on all sides of the religious divides and of children embodying the project as a direct result of our interventions. That said, however, I do believe that the feelings I experienced on my first visit still exist in varying concentrations, despite having visited four times by 2005. Being born and brought up in England, where war and conflict are not on your doorstep, where you know violence, death and volatility are not commonplace in parts of the country, I feel you just have an inherent mind set. This mind set is going to come to the fore to a greater or lesser extent when entering into an environment that contrasts greatly with the one you have always known. This can cause dissonance and lead to these feelings. Obviously with positive experiences and accessing knowledge to the contrary such feelings become less pronounced, but never eliminated. Also, I have learnt over time that it would be both naïve and wrong to become complacent and forget that Israel can be a dangerous and volatile country.

Using previous experiences to resolve conflict is incredibly easy when you are thrown together with so many warm and hospitable people. At every social engagement attended, you are greeted with welcoming, open arms. It often feels as if the communities want to show their appreciation for what the project is trying to achieve, and show us their support for the project as a whole and for the individuals within it, working to ensure it was a success. At times I have felt honoured to be welcomed so openly into the communities. At such times I often felt a tinge of guilt that I have had to overcome negative thoughts to be there at all. This overwhelming hospitality is probably most overt when it comes to meal times.

Dining is a very important social vehicle in Arab communities. Meals tend to last for hours as discussion meanders, decisions are made, plans are hatched. There tend to be vague protocols that are loosely adhered to. The basic format is that every imaginable salad-type dish is served with mountains of pita bread and dollops of humus. At this stage the seasoned guest moderates their eating in readiness for the arrival of mountains of freshly prepared meat, rice and vegetable dishes. Hungry students, first-time coaches gorge themselves and shift uncomfortably as they realise they have misjudged the full extent of the banquet as the main course arrives. What commonly ensues is one of the more light hearted clashes of cultures that we witness during F4P projects. This is the battle between polite, young British coaches who have been educated on the basis that leaving food will be construed as rude by your host, and the Arab host who prides himself on the wealth and variety of his hospitality. Should you succeed in clearing your plate he will be embarrassed and consider himself as a poor host on the basis that he was not able to adequately provide for his guests. This has been a recurrent theme. It is evident that the richness of the dining provided

by our hosts represents a form of reciprocity for our work in bringing F4P
to their communities. I felt this hospitality and wonderful treatment we
experienced each evening was a representation of the communities' support,
appreciation and recognition for the work everyone within the project was
doing. It was one very obvious way of showing how welcome we are and the
desire of the community to be part of the project and help continue its
development.

Since being involved in F4P my view of Israel has rarely been static.
There is so much to learn and appreciate that every day of every visit is filled
with opportunities to gather knowledge and first hand experience of one of
the most historical and culturally diverse regions of the world. This diversity
is part of the problem. The whole notion of co-existence relies upon
individuals observing and respecting cultural differences. As each year
unfolded I have been able to become acutely aware of many such differences,
some of which were interesting to behold, others were more difficult to
comprehend and threatened my ability to uphold the F4P value of neutrality.

Whilst interesting and valuable to analyse, the differences between Arab
and Jewish hospitality and food are superficial and unimportant in the
context of other differences witnessed. These differences can soon be viewed
as inequalities and then injustices if emotion goes unchecked. I have become
increasingly aware of a far more significant and glaringly stark contrast
between the communities. Driving around the country en route to our
coaching venues, within our venues and when visiting communities it is easy
to notice how the Jewish communities are often characterised by tree lined
suburban streets, parks, large shopping centres, organised and well kept
housing estates and kibbutzim. In contrast, in a typical Arab community,
you would find many half built houses, small corner shops, seemingly
unplanned and unregulated town construction with degenerating roads
and areas of apparent wasteland with rubble and large rocks. Often, the only
piece of well maintained land is the football pitch we were using. Arab
towns seemed to be located in less accessible terrain with poorer transport
networks and less evidence of public amenities such as road sweeping and
street lighting. I have often found myself becoming increasingly agitated
about this and have found it difficult to understand and comprehend that
communities, in the same country, in some cases maybe only a few miles
apart, exist with such an explicit level of inequality. The need for 'living the
values' and specifically the value of neutrality was clear in such
circumstances.

This situation is clearly of a far greater magnitude than we can ever envisage addressing through a football project. However, one example of addressing inequality on an individual level, which has been another recurring theme that I have tried to confront on every F4P project, is embedded in the system of translation used in coaching sessions. Within the football camps each UK coach works alongside a Jewish and Arab local coach, thus enabling clear translation of instructions to the children in both Hebrew and Arabic. Within this three-way working relationship an interesting sequence of events often emerges. This then becomes something to question and change. After the coach finishes speaking and allows the local coaches to translate, the Jewish coach always seems to go first and take the lead, be the dominant voice almost. With some local coaches in certain camps this situation is more pronounced than with others, but in all cases it seemed to be the general pattern. The Arab coaches are constantly encouraged to take the initiative and even a rotation system was tried to ensure the Arab coach took an equal turn at speaking first and was an equal 'presence' within the session. However, this is often very difficult as on occasions it seems the Arab coaches are actually reluctant themselves to take on an equal role within the session.

Whilst trying to avoid ill-informed conclusions, I continued at all times to try to tackle this issue when it occurred. The common explanation of this sequence of translation is that the Arab coaches need to hear the Hebrew translation first and then translate from the Hebrew as Arabs speak both Hebrew and Arabic. Jewish coaches have a better grasp of English and do not speak Arabic as there is no obligation for them to learn the language at any stage of their education. Whilst this explanation served, to a limited extent, to placate my perception of one equality it nurtured another: Arabs must learn Hebrew, and Jews do not need to learn Arabic. Of similar impact in terms of inequality is the extent to which impartial on-lookers can often identify children from different communities, not by their appearance or even their name but by the nature and quality of their clothes and training shoes, with the Jewish children usually being in superior kit. Another key feature of F4P in combating this socially engineered inequality is the provision of uniform F4P training shirts to every child thus ensuring equality and neutrality. These significant experiences and moments I have touched upon are ones I consider crucial in developing my understanding of the country and forming a foundation to work from. They represent constant discovery and the learning and gathering of information in many different respects. In hindsight these experiences have enabled me to feel confident, knowledgeable and prepared for the ever evolving challenge of the F4P project.

The heart and soul of F4P is what happens on the coaching ground. Immediately striking is the speed at which the UK and Israeli coaches form relationships, possibly due to the nature of the shared situation and the shared goals and values that each of us hold as individuals. However, this does not always guarantee that a genuine friendship and understanding will be formed between individuals. In my case, the relationships formed were clearly genuine and heartfelt from both parties and they are relationships built on mutual respect, trust and appreciation. The football sessions with the children benefit enormously from these relationships formed between the coaches. It allows the sessions to be more productive, enjoyable and free flowing, with an atmosphere of understanding and co-operation, which is exactly what we try to foster amongst the children. The status as adults being role models for the children is underlined in this instance. The common image of politicians and religious figureheads castigating each other cannot be in the best interests of the next generation of Israelis. The ongoing need for adults themselves to 'live the values' by showing mutual respect and respect of each others' opinions and faith is of a high priority. This notion has been equally important for subsequent groups of UK coaches to observe. There can be no place for compromising the values by not representing the content of the F4P manual. The human behaviours contained within should be adhered to on and off the football pitch at all times.

My experiences as a coach for F4P have never been so fraught or stress-ridden as the preparation for my first ever training session. As I travelled to my first coaching session on the I'blin pitch I remember just contemplating the potential challenges that lay ahead. I'blin is an Arab town and its pitches appear to be the only piece of well-maintained, rubble free, green grass for miles around. The stadium sits between two high hills on either side, each one dotted with stone houses, rocks, trees and shrubs. The stadium walls are high, with barbed wire lining the top of some sections, giving it something of a prison feel. At that point, in 2002, everything in Israel was a completely new experience for me and, as in this case, many thoughts, some perhaps irrational, would flash through my mind on encountering things for the first time. The coaching was undoubtedly going to be the most important and significant of these new experiences. At the core of the project are its central aims and values, and the coaching 'on the ground' is all about encouraging and imparting these values, hence its centrality to F4P. Trying not to be too nervous I was thinking of issues that could arise out of the fact that translation was required, the importance of emphasising the values and not 'just playing football' and the environmental conditions such as the heat. Also, I had persistent questions playing in my mind. Would these children take to me, respond to me as a UK coach in their country? Would they even listen to me, or worse still, would they respect or like me? There were many unknown features and uncontrollable features of the environment I was heading for. With the benefit of hindsight many of these feelings were indeed irrational, but what became apparent is the extent to which my anxieties had completely swung from worrying about being in a potentially dangerous and alien environment to generic issues related to coaching pedagogy.

When I look back I think of how quickly on that first coaching day I realised how responsive and enthusiastic the children were to the presence of a UK coach. This first experience epitomised the concept of a steep learning curve and one which resides firmly in my data base of positive thoughts when having to deal with future conflicts concerning involvement in F4P. It was the encouraging and imparting of the values through the football that was always of most concern to me and this has not changed with each subsequent year. I wanted to ensure as much as I could that I was doing everything possible to clearly emphasise the significance of these values, using football as the medium, whilst ensuring that every child was having fun and displaying the values through playing. In working to achieve this, the F4P coaching manual was invaluable. I believe its inception in 2004 was a huge step forward for F4P. It provided the structure and guidance to the sessions. It gave every coach confidence as they could easily follow and use the manual and build upon it with any of their own ideas. In a situation unfamiliar and challenging for other reasons it was crucial to have some stability, created by the manual, within the coaching aspect of the project. Projecting my thoughts to the future, the manual is an invaluable and innovative tool which has the potential to transfer to any number of different sports or cultures.

F4P is not about coaching football drills or activities in order to develop technique. If a child improves her/his level of skill it is a bonus and that is all. F4P is about the values, football is the medium. It is important to talk to the children for a few minutes at the start of each session about the particular value for that day — for example, trust and what it means, how it can be shown in society and how it is important in a football context. The major challenge is then to create football based scenarios where the values can be exemplified and celebrated. Recognising the values as they arise and being able to manipulate practices in an attempt to bring out the values are on-going professional challenges that I have been constantly trying to develop as F4P matures.

As a coach it is a great feeling to observe a clear example of a value being displayed by the children. Positive behaviour by a child, demonstrating a value however small, is a very important moment and represented the deepest core of the F4P project. It has great significance for the project as a whole but also for the individual coach working with those children. As a coach it is so encouraging and motivating. It gives you immense confidence in your coaching techniques and your ability to communicate and form relationships with the children. As coaches we are asked to identify and highlight these examples of positive behaviours to the children, and these instances are referred to as 'teachable moments', clear examples amongst the children where a value has been displayed. This further reinforces the importance of the value to the children and encourages it to be repeated and more importantly remembered.

I am sure that each project is blessed with numerous examples of instances where the F4P manual and its values have come alive with the behaviour of the children. I can recall numerous heart-warming moments from every year of my involvement. These instances are the real high points of F4P. These are the key moments which justify the emotional conflict and the hours spent preparing for the project. These are the moments which fuel the enthusiasm and the belief that the project works and fulfils a vital role in young lives. I witnessed one such example on the immaculate training pitch in Nazareth. The children were revelling in playing on it. We had begun a match to finish the coaching session and a young Jewish boy, a skilful player, was running with the ball, evading tackles, twisting and turning, cutting in and out until he finally unleashed an unstoppable shot that flew into the top corner. Everyone just stood and watched as it nestled in the back of the net. The next scene was of every player on the pitch, Arab and Jew, celebrating with the Jewish boy, congratulating him, shaking his hand, patting him on the back and hoisting him up. The Jewish boy looked overcome with emotion, partly due to the fact that he will probably never score a better goal again in his life but undoubtedly also because of the reaction of the other children. I'm sure he won't forget that moment and in the context of the project it was fantastic for me and the local coaches to witness.

In contrast to these emotional highs there are the moments when you are left questioning the worth of the project as situations arise where the values are rejected and sometimes ignored. These instances sometimes feature the actions of children on the training ground when they are overcome by competition or drive to win. More worryingly these instances have involved parents and coaches who fail to observe the politics-free zone surrounding F4P. With time I discovered that these problems are likely to face every student coach. These are often issues which are very difficult to resolve because of the nature of the situation in which we are working. When problems and conflict arise amongst the children within a coaching session, specifically between a Jewish and Arab child, or when a child seems to be openly rejecting the values through his behaviour, it is difficult for a coach to know how to interpret this. Given the nature of the environment it is easy to view such incidents as symptomatic of the divided society and the inherent conflict within the nation. Indeed, this may have been the case. However, I have often felt I have to be wary of imposing a more sinister explanation on a scenario that may have a much simpler and less disturbing one. It may just be the fact that as in the UK, or anywhere for that matter, when coaching children there may be those who are difficult to deal with and who are more disruptive and awkward. Sometimes children simply don't get on, irrespective of wider issues of identity. This is a reality, but in this case it is potentially obscured and overlooked because of the circumstances in which we find ourselves as coaches. It is often important to remember that kids are kids before they are given any religious identity and therefore always likely to fall out and argue on occasions. As for adults, the same can be said in that there will always be idiots regardless of religious persuasion. At no time was this more apparent than on the training ground in 2005. I had progressed to project leader and was confronted with one Arab and one Jewish parent who had taken as instant dislike for one another due to a petty disagreement concerning access to the training pitch. Diffusing a potential explosive situation gave me a strong sense of satisfaction but at the same time signalled the start of a period of interrogation of why we even bother with F4P.

On many occasions I have found myself and other coaches becoming somewhat disheartened after encountering problems with the children. It is sometimes difficult to know the best way to tackle incidents. At times such as this it is important to remember that the role we are undertaking is far from an easy one. To encourage and impart the values of the project to the children through the football, whilst trying to control the natural emotions and attitudes, such as competitiveness and aggression that can characterise football is a difficult challenge. Even given this challenge the positive behaviours, the 'teachable moments', often seem to far outweigh the negative experiences being witnessed. This is the important fact for everyone to recognise; on balance a coach can expect many more highs than lows.

I have often considered the notion that coaches can make too great an emotional investment in F4P. The vast majority of coaches seem to take huge pride in their personal slice of F4P. They see themselves as guardians of the project for the year and as a result see themselves as taking responsibility for its well-being. When situations or children conspire against you it is easy to become downhearted because of this emotional attachment. Simply not investing emotionally is not an option as all who have made the decision to take part in F4P had gone through similar processes of justifying their involvement in the face of one-dimensional media coverage and probing questions from people at home. My conclusion is that this is part of the success of F4P. People care passionately about it and take immense pride in being associated with it. This emotion also comes through loud and clear to children, parents and community coaches and is often very well reciprocated.

Being promoted to project leader for the 2005 project was a challenging but welcome experience. As with any change of perspective I was able to view the project differently and as a result new and different issues came to my attention. Now that I was in a different position of responsibility it was very interesting to approach it from a leadership perspective and tackle particular problems and incidents. I soon realised the importance of diplomacy and being a negotiator. I wasn't so 'hands on' in terms of the football and had less interaction with the children compared to previous years in a coaching capacity. However, as a leader I found myself at different times needing to offer advice and support, being at the centre of conversations or exchanges between local volunteers, sometimes needing to be a mediating presence, and generally ensuring the project ran smoothly and was the best it could be. Given the nature of the situation I found my previous experience was critical. It gave me confidence and belief and no doubt enabled me to cope.

I have found that one of the most important roles as a leader was listening to the feelings of the other coaches within my group. These were experienced coaches in the UK, but who were working with F4P for the first time and encountering some problems and issues in the context of the project. I could still recall the anxieties of coming to Israel for the first time, dealing with the conflict in my head and then coping with the stress of delivering a values-based coaching project for the first time. I felt very well prepared to empathise with the coaches and offer the assistance and reassurance they needed.

When considering the future for the F4P project I feel there could be a tendency to view things in an idealistic way by suggesting that the project will always continue to improve, grow and develop, hence I am very wary of doing this. I want to believe that this will be the case and hopefully the project will go from strength to strength. I feel for the sake of everyone involved in the project, and also for everyone it has touched since its inception, no matter how briefly, that F4P must continue to grow and develop. I feel the children of Israel within the communities where we have worked, and for any new communities wishing to come on board, must have the opportunity to be involved in the project, embrace it and benefit from it. Furthermore, as a student volunteer who has gained so much through my involvement, I firmly believe the next generation of prospective UK student volunteers must have the chance to gain the personal development I have gained through experiences in Israel and the F4P project.

When considering the impact of F4P and evidence that our work has any efficacy in the communities in which we have been working we can look towards the outcomes of long-term qualitative research. In terms of the short term I am left to consider the likely impact of 5 days of coaching, once a year. I think of the continuity of the project in the absence of the UK team and the likelihood that our partners in Israel will carry forward the momentum from the F4P coaching weeks. The more enduring legacy is images of Arab and Jewish children swapping mobile phone numbers and email addresses and of community leaders arranging friendly fixtures with their new 'friends'. In some instances communities have continued the F4P themes relating to breaking gender divides and have introduced their own female teams. These anecdotes are far removed from the big picture of peace in the Middle East but immeasurable in the lives of the people concerned.

Continuing the theme of impact, F4P has left its mark on me with memories, experiences, challenges and so much more. At the beginning of my involvement with the project I did not think that four years later I would be reflecting on it in this way. The most significant thing I can say is that I now see myself as a different person from the one who stepped on Israir flight 107 to Israel for the first time in 2002. The project, with its central aims and values, has done some highly significant work through the dedication of the UK staff and Israeli partners. I believe the F4P project has and will continue to make an ever increasing and significant contribution to working towards conflict resolution and achieving peaceful co-existence within Israel. Concluding my personal point of view, as the project has developed and changed over the years so have I, in terms of my confidence, coaching techniques, understanding of the country and my ability to work with the children and local coaches. All these things have inevitably improved through constantly learning, experiencing and actively trying to gain as much information and advice as possible. In this respect, I feel my entire time on the F4P project has been invaluable to my development as a human being. Some of the skills and knowledge I have attained and situations I have been exposed to will stay with me for the rest of my life. I have no doubt there will be times in the future when I will be thankful for them. It is largely because of this that I feel privileged and lucky to have experienced this long term involvement and to have had the opportunity to grow and develop as the project has done likewise. Completing the circle, in the context of F4P, I feel I can say without doubt that I have stayed true to my philosophy of making the most of my University life.

Chapter 9

FOOTBALL FOR PEACE.
A PHYSICAL EDUCATION TEACHER'S
PERSPECTIVE

Stuart Townsend[1]

The success of a community is largely dependent upon how external forces act upon it and how internal forces act within it. This basic concept is never far from the agenda in the everyday life of a school teacher. The hierarchical nature of education in the UK is very apparent with the omnipresence of external agencies pushing from all angles to raise achievement and the quality of teaching and learning. The cynics among us may argue that the cascade of policy and bureaucracy is tantamount to coercion and a fixation to create a controlled workforce. The extent of this control has been criticised in that it may endanger the autonomy, flexibility and spontaneity of the education process and result in a production line of clones that have been assessed, graded, monitored and moderated at every turn. The micro community of education, the school, is dependent upon its staff and students to translate and apply policy to the best of their capability and resources.

The English education system is largely governed by the delivery of the National Curriculum in all subjects, including the delivery of Physical Education (PE). The existence of the guidelines contained within can be argued positive or negative in the quest for greater physical literacy, health and social and moral development. What is less debatable is that school autonomy is becoming increasingly restricted in the quest for higher standards of academic attainment. The educational process is also being subjected to increased pressure in pursuit of the same goals. One of the key attractions of returning to the Football for Peace (F4P) project for me and my colleagues at Dorothy Stringer[2] was to identify the potential for raising the status of values based teaching and learning in physical education lessons. For us it was the opportunity to get back to basics in a move to shift some of the emphasis away from performance and back to the humanistic roots of PE.

Regardless of the environment, the basic rules for the success of a community are applicable. The communities of Menashe and Kafa Qara independently mirrored this picture. Within the big picture of Israel it is clear that both communities have widely contrasting circumstances in which to operate. One, Menashe, is a Jewish town of typical appearance and demographic; the other, Kafa Qara, is a typically bustling Arab town of random architecture. Taking a closer look, they had remarkably similar infrastructures in which to build thriving and supportive communities. Both communities are open and accepting of the concept of co-existence and could point towards cross sections of their communities where co-existence goes unnoticed, such is its ritualised status. Both communities are supported by proactive individuals who welcome the concept of F4P. They treated us like their own for the duration of our stay. My concluding thought on the nature of our partners for the 2005 project was that the external, uncontrollable powers that exist in the complex political structure of Israel clearly make life very challenging for these communities but the internal, positive forces are vibrant, enthusiastic and willing to make a success out of the hand that they have been dealt.

Kafa Qara is an Arab town situated south west of Nazareth and is approximately 3 miles from the border of the West Bank. The town openly promotes and accepts coexistence between Arabs and Jews. There is often a difference between reality and rhetoric in Israel but in this instance it was clear that co-existence was all around us. Given this progressive societal picture it was clear that F4P would not be breaking new ground. We would be assimilating into an already welcoming community with many of the traditional barriers to F4P posing less of a concern. One of the key personnel in Kara Qara was Yusif Asali. Yusif works very closely with the local council in providing sport and recreational activities for the local children. Due to the fact that the community are promoting co-existence between Arabs and Jews, there are already numerous projects going on in Kfar Qara that involve local children, such as cycling days out in the forest, BBQs and other food celebrations. Yusif showed us a collection of photographs from these events and he was obviously very proud of what the community is achieving, but as always Yusif is striving to expand these projects so that more individuals are touched by what the council is trying to achieve. With this in mind, the local football teams already have Arabic and Jewish children playing alongside each other in the same teams. There were 50 names of children put down to take part in the Football 4 Peace project, but Yusif explained to us that he could easily double the number of children that would participate if the project expanded and allowed the community to provide the project to more children. I was very pleasantly surprised to see that the community were striving to make co-existence a success because I had expected lots of opposition from local residents who were not in support of what we were trying to achieve. I found this concept very appealing, particularly in light of the expectations placed on specialist sports colleges in the UK[3] who have a remit to provide positive experiences for the community as a whole. The role undertaken by Yusif was multi-dimensional and, it seemed, not too far removed from that of a UK sports development officer with its mix of education, sport and local government involvement. I immediately drew parallels with the current role of School Sport Co-ordinators who are housed in schools and yet work within a complex web of sport and physical activity providers. My reflections also concluded that there seems to be an existing infrastructure in place in the UK to engage a little closer with the community and to break the traditional focus of schools working as a 'closed shop' and to increase cross-community provisions.

Our Jewish community was Kibbutz Menashe which is situated only 2–3 miles away from its Arab neighbours. Our guide and leader was Haim Nadler who works on the kibbutz and runs the local youth football team. The local youth team is linked with Maccabi Tel Aviv, which is one of the popular professional teams of Israel. The playing field is situated at the very beginning of the Kibbutz and is easily visible from the road. The children from the Kibbutz wear the Maccabi Tel Aviv training kit which is yellow and blue. The office which runs the club has posters, banners and pictures of both Jewish and Arab players spread all over the walls and doors with the colours of yellow and blue prominently showing for all to see. Haim Nadler explained to us that it is very important that there are local clubs, such as this one in Menashe, that are supported by professional clubs. This means that the children have players and role models to aspire to and it gives them 'ownership' as they will be proud of the fact that they are part of the Maccabi Tel Aviv club structure.

The concept of role model status is one which is liberally thrown around when discussion moves to children and sport. We are very familiar in the UK with the anecdotes that are attached to professional football and the potential for encouraging dysfunctional behaviour. Here was a bigger statement relating to role model status. Maccabi Tel Aviv are a Jewish team but publicly represent a model of co-existence. They recruit players from a range of communities and their team is made of both Arabs and Jews. The messages here were clear and act as high profile model for clubs across the country to try to emulate. The use of the Macaabi Tel Aviv brand therefore does not alienate any sections of the community and provides a stimulus for the impressionable youth to follow. However, this can sometimes seem idealistic and in some cases results fall short of expectations. An article in *The Sunday Times* (March 20, 2005), highlighted the problems with racism at games, with players experiencing abuse from not only rival fans but also home supporters. In one such game an Arabic player left the field of play in tears after suffering racial abuse from his own supporters. However, is this far from the degree of sectarian abuse in some cites in the UK or even from the abuse endured by black players in 'civilised' European countries?

I have experienced Israel in two different capacities, one as a coach in my first year of involvement with the project and the second year as a group leader. These two experiences have given me the chance to see the effect of the Israeli coaches on the children who have been coached in the communities. As I progressed from coach to project leader I became increasingly aware of the coaching styles that were being adopted in search of the values. From a position of experience I could reflect on the huge shift of focus from issues relating to oneself to a focus on the children and the tasks they were undertaking. I could reflect on my own initial teaching experiences where anxiety was almost completely focused on my own performance. Would they listen to me? Would they behave themselves? How do I sound? What should I do next? These were the sum total of my thoughts.

With time and increased self assurance the focus could move to more practical and environmental concerns relating to the climate of the coaching sessions. This phenomenon was also highly evident during my teaching practices and my first year as a teacher. I considered that humanistic values, for example respect, would automatically occur as part of the progression of PE lessons. However, taking an analytical perspective on F4P I have questioned whether there is an increased demand for the inclusion of more formal values based teaching and learning in order to ensure that we are educating socially and morally astute individuals who do not try to win at all costs and have respect for others.

Through my involvement with F4P I have been able to gain a wide range of knowledge in how the concept of values based teaching can be easily promoted into an English PE curriculum. We already know the disproportional emphasis placed on standards and exam success, so any curriculum innovation which takes time for this pursuit is unlikely to be sanctioned by many schools. However, the subtle and totally unobtrusive mode of delivery of the F4P material and its values of neutrality, trust, responsibility, respect and inclusion provides an excellent medium for the imparting of desirable behaviours. The F4P manual contains drills and practices which would feature in any invasion games scheme of work at Key Stage 3. There is little new or innovative about the physical content. However, the recommended methodology is the key to its success. It is much less about the 'what' and more about the 'how'. In this respect F4P can be classified as a hybrid between teaching and coaching, concerning itself much more with the process rather than the product. The pivotal choices revolve around the teaching styles employed by the coach. Predominant teaching styles employed are ones which allowed a greater extent of social interaction, decision-making, player autonomy and problem solving. The major theory here is the engagement in dialogue in pursuit of common goals, setting aside personal differences to achieve a desired outcome. The coaches are encouraged to design practices which are suitably open-ended, or likely to result in controversy or debate. The coach then adopt the role of mediator between the two sides until they find solutions to the problem or resolutions to arguments.

I believe it is possible to adopt a more open-ended style of delivery which asks social and moral questions of the children without compromising the content aspect of lessons. During coaching days on F4P I was able to construct and solidify this belief by watching the process unfold. As a coaching team we identified key practices within each session where we could predict that each of the values would emerge. We looked at the conditions placed on games and the organisation of competitive practices and could make educated assertions that certain events would unfold thus preparing ourselves for a well informed plenary session on how children responded to situations as they arose. Examples of such conditions included playing games with no referees and standing firm when disagreements emerged. The players would soon make honest decisions when they realised that game time was being wasted while they argued over possession at a throw in. Games were played in silence where all forms of non-verbal communication were practised, a condition which sparks a wider discussion on 'speaking without words'. Demonstrations were often used to identify good technique but more often to demonstrate behaviours which embodied the values such as shaking hands, congratulating an opponent or collecting their ball after a wayward shot at goal. The plenary at the end of each session revolved around the discussion of these instances of positive behaviour and representations of neutrality, trust, responsibility, respect and inclusion. Children were rarely left to wonder about how to catch the eye of the UK coaches or how to be rewarded with a warm smile, pat on the back or a celebratory round of applause. The children were well aware of what success on F4P meant and how they could feel successful. The absence of tangible rewards further served to enhance the intrinsic nature of the project and avoided any notion of extrinsic rewards in pursuit of positive behaviours.

The notion of a reward system is one which is highly visible in the life of every school and familiar to all teachers. This seeps into the schools' psyche in many forms from certificates, medals and notes home in dairies to the more subtle messages of pictures of sports teams, house captains and trophy winners. School awards almost exclusively celebrate the most outstanding attainment or most likely to do well. All of this is the result of a society which is clear in its meritocratic philosophy. I was left to ponder the last time I gave tangible or non tangible encouragement to a child for simply displaying positive human characteristics or the last time I congratulated a child for merely persevering or improving. It is unfair to suggest that this does not occur, it clearly does but it would be foolish to consider that there is not a huge imbalance in favour of celebrating outcomes over process. The way in which we view rewards does not have to compromise the content of lessons, the attainment or any children or the drive for results. Neither would it change or inhibit any of the 'quality' issues which dictate much of the remit of modern schools. The provision of a clear pathway and greater flexibility in what we deem to be success and changing children's perceptions of success would communicate completely different messages to many more children. The end product may even create an environment where children begin to ritualise the kinds of behaviours that we routinely see on F4P projects.

Progressing to the role of project leader gave me a greater opportunity to analyse the processes adopted by coaches. The support I could offer was initially based on my previous year as a coach and I felt I could easily empathise with the coaches in what they were trying to achieve. The coaching manual was a key document in supporting the work of coaches.

It not only provides informative drills and content ideas but it provides a clear methodology to the coaching and insights into how to create the right environment for 'teachable moments'. The manual provides a framework within which to base sessions and a source for reference. It also provides consistency to an ever-growing number of projects. It is the constant in an ever changing environment. In this respect I was able to draw similarities with the National Curriculum for Physical Education (NCPE) which provides the consistent framework which schools can, within certain parameters, tailor to their own specifications. The manual offers many of the same concepts as the NCPE but, thankfully, avoids much of the jargon and many educational 'buzz' phrases.

The NCPE demands a range of open-ended teaching styles in order for pupils to select and apply skills and ideas in a range of settings. Children are required to be put into situations where they are able to evaluate and improve their own and others' performances. Within these strands of the NCPE I could easily visualise many of the processes being engaged in by children and coaches in F4P. The styles of divergent and guided discovery are popular when asking children to select and apply in UK schools, and the same styles were being demonstrated by the F4P coaches encouraging children to overcome the problem of working out their own substitutions in a fair and equitable fashion. The styles of reciprocal- and self-check are very popular in UK schools in creating occasions where children can analyse and feedback on the progress of themselves and others. The same styles were being ably applied by F4P coaches when encouraging a sharing of technical or tactical ideas or when children were given control of the group for 5 minutes at a time to demonstrate responsibility. The underlying reasons for these teaching styles and modes of learning correlate very clearly. However, it can easily be argued that the prevailing reasons for using these styles are fundamentally different. In the school context they are likely to be motivated by gains in knowledge and performance, whereas F4P is focused clearly on the process and subsequent personal value that these teaching styles offer.

In my role as a leader, a slightly more withdrawn role than direct coaching, more similarities between this environment and teaching in the UK became apparent, such as the importance of role models. If the coach or teacher is upbeat, positive and encourageing, then the pupils react in a positive manner by trying to portray these values and aspire to act the way that the role model does. The role model must use a combination of verbal and non-verbal mannerisms to portray him/herself in a positive light. Pupils will react depending on these verbal and non-verbal actions and thus will portray these actions both in and out of school. It a large assumption and in some ways rather idealistic, but the concept of initiating positive behaviour on the football pitch that can then be taken into society is a fundamental goal of the project. In many ways this is similar to the way in which the use of citizenship and values based teaching attempts to encourage the transfer of these habits into the school as a whole and then into the wider society. With some minor exceptions, F4P coaches seemed to understand this vital aspect of their role and upheld these values throughout their work.

It is currently very apparent that many young footballers use unacceptable language on the football field towards both players and officials, which could be due to the fact that many role models in professional football can be seen at times to use language that could be classed as foul and abusive on the football pitch. It is unsurprising that these instances are often carried off the pitch into their everyday lives. The choice of football for a values based coaching project can be considered ironic given the nature of the current corruption and gamesmanship that surrounds it in just about every part of the globe! Upon reflection, it can be seen that as values are being eroded in football they are also being eroded in pockets of society in the UK and in Israel. Projects such as F4P must be empowered to take a role in reversing this trend in football as well the community as a whole.

I found influencing coaching styles and recommending how material is presented a relatively straightforward process once I had made a shift into UK PE teacher mode. I had identified similarities in the way I view my role as a PE teacher and as a project leader on F4P and could therefore advise less-experienced practitioners as if I was mentoring them on teaching practice and they were teaching a lesson which required the fulfilment of several personal and social lesson objectives. A key development in the success of the Kafa Qara/Menashe project was the move to a greater emphasis on teaching through the game and whole-part-whole teaching where the emphasis starts on the game, an element is isolated and worked on and then fed back into a conditioned game. Whilst teaching at school I often use a whole-part-whole teaching approach as this frequently proves to be a successful way of engaging pupils from the very start of lessons, hence they are excited and energy levels are increased. With energy levels high, it is then easier to break down larger skills into smaller skills.

As a coaching team, we felt after the first two days of coaching that our groups of children were not really engaging with each other the way that we would have liked. We concluded that the way we presented the tasks was a key consideration. We decided to adopt a strategy similar to the whole-part-whole teaching approach where we would start the session with warm-up and trust exercises and then go straight into a game, which we felt was the area where the pupils were showing most engagement in the F4P key values. After the initial game, we then went into the skills and drills part of the session and then finished with a final game to ensure that all of the values learnt in that day's session were being used by the children. This approach also would give us a basis to explain the teachable moments by using situations from the initial games. Children were given time to reflect on how they responded to situations and could discuss more appropriate strategies if the same situation present itself in the next game. This style of delivery, particularly when paired with unobtrusive refereeing of games, is very challenging. Teachers and coaches are traditionally programmed to spot weakness in techniques and tactics and to use their critical eye and expert knowledge to improve the outcome. This urge was clearly strong in all of the coaches, including myself, but the essence of the F4P philosophy lies in the children themselves solving disputes and overcoming hurdles as they arise.

Once they had overcome their urge to be more heavily involved in the educational process the coaches used the new tactics and we were astonished at how effective the new strategies proved to be. The initial games played meant that the children had to interact and almost learn through their own mistakes because the coaches stood back and watched from the sidelines and gave no refereeing or instructional input. I have since used this type of feedback in my lessons whilst umpiring or refereeing games and it has worked on many occasions. However, it does not work when there are too many dominant aggressive children in the group because they tend to influence the quieter children into submission. In this instance the coach or teacher is then tested to use strategies to empower all children to have a voice in the decision-making process. I was left to reflect on how fulfilling these sessions had been for both the children and the coaches. My second thought was directed towards how a government assessor (OFSTED) would grade such a lesson where no teaching points had been given and almost no direction or organisation was undertaken by the coach.

A visit to the schools in Kafa Qara provided a key opportunity for me to gather some further insights into the community. We visited a local primary school that had been built by the British army in 1947 before Israel was formed as the country we see today on global maps. The school was built for the local community so that children could be educated. The foundations of the school still remain today. The school has since expanded and extensions have been built onto the existing structure. Inside, the school classrooms were awash with colour and vibrancy, with posters everywhere the eye could see. Many classrooms had English words posted on the wall as well as numbers and short 3-4 letter words in order to display the letters of the alphabet. In addition to this there was a mixture of Hebrew and Arabic words, which showed that the school encourage coexistence between the different sections of Israeli society. At Dorothy Stringer High School, there is a philosophy that the learning environment should be an integral part of the pupils' learning. The walls are designed to promote inclusion with pictures and examples of a wide range of sports performers. Ability, disability, race and gender are all represented which sends a much more inclusive message to children than the more typical displays of sports team excellence that says little about the process of PE. This philosophy was evident in Kafa Qara as the hidden messages promoting inclusion were clearly evident. The learning environment represented the school population with a healthy balance between Arabic, Jewish and English words, symbols and images. The concept of inclusion was clear, albeit inclusion across different groups of society to those in the UK.

The environment I had witnessed further supported the notion of inclusion that we practice in the UK and was at odds with my stereotypical expectation that I would see patriotic displays around the school representing only one side of society, in this case the Arab cause. I had half expected to see a prominent divide in the hidden curriculum of schools in Jewish and Arab towns with celebrations of ideological identity, much the same as is commonly seen in the USA with constant representation of the Stars and Stripes in classrooms.

There was another very powerful symbol of coexistence in the school reception area, a picture of Yitzhak Rabin. I was astounded by this. A picture of a former Israeli Prime Minster in a school in an Arab town was not consistent the image portrayed by Western media. Rabin was key political figure and was seen as a great hope for the peaceful future of Israel and in the provision of a Palestinian state. He was assassinated in 1995 by a Jewish extremist who saw his concessions to the Arabs as too great a sacrifice. I reflected upon what this primary school might teach to their pupils in history lessons and whether there is a degree of bias in how the last 60 years are portrayed— after all, the history books in the UK do not enter into any real detail about the barbarism of colonial rule. With a sense of vanity I also considered whether there would one day be mention of the involvement of Football 4 Peace in the local community.

As well as the primary school, there are another two secondary schools in Kfar Qara. One of the secondary schools is purely for Arab children, but the other school, I was surprised to learn, is attended by both Arab and Jewish children. The physical environment was a further extension of the inclusive nature of the primary school. This was very tangible proof that co-existence can work with children who are taught sitting together side by side at desks, hence mixing on a daily basis and making friends with children and sweeping ideological differences aside. My reflections were with the types of teachers who work in such schools and the training they must have received. My time at the University of Brighton was underpinned by the notion of total inclusive practice but would have in no way prepared me for the inclusion required in a mixed Arab and Jewish school. How did teachers juggle there teaching around the various religious festivals? How did grouping policies reflect Arab conventions regarding girls and physical activity? Do these teachers teach the same values that the Football 4 peace Project promotes? How was history and sociology taught? Many questions, some potentially controversial, but the overriding principle was that here was a very real and thriving model of co-existence. This political statement made by the council is a very powerful statement sent out for the rest of the community to take note of the values that they wish to be embedded into the children of Kafa Qara and the surrounding communities. The only downside from my very selfish perspective was that the children were on their school summer holidays so I did not get a chance to observe this model in action.

As the children were on their summer break the community provided for them and kept them entertained during the day. F4P was one of these organised activities. A full programme of summer activities kept the children active and engaged during the days while their parents were at work. Whilst entertaining the children the messages of F4P were constantly promoted. A recurring issue when discussing F4P is its continuity and whether projects practice co-existence following on from the 5 days of F4P activity. The hub of activity in Kafa Qara and Menashe suggested that the use of co-existence activities were in good health and actively supported by a cross section of the communities. Singing, painting and swimming were just some of the other projects that we witnessed during our time in Israel.

In the UK there are many times in lessons when pupils show disregard towards others in the form of bullying and aggressive behaviour, but what causes these behavious? The majority of squabbles are over minor issues arising in small friendship groups and reveal no sustainable or substantial evidence for such bad feeling, yet it happens on a regular basis. Many pupils find it hard to mix with others in their classes and often refuse to work and co-operate with their peers, meaning that there are often pupils left isolated when pupils are left to choose small groups to work with in lessons. If the Football 4 Peace project can help bring children together from diverse communities where there is sustained hatred and divides created due to religious beliefs, then it is intuitively appealing to suggest that there are strategies from the F4P manual that PE teachers can use to try to eradicate bullying and ill feeling between pupils in the UK.

Coaching in Israel over the last 2 years has changed the way that I look at my personal teaching career. It is clearly evident that the issues faced by Israel on a macro level are not experienced in England. But when we look at the relationship between schools in England and schools in Israel there are clear similarities in the way that the communities operate and educate, and it is not unrealistic to suggest that the philosophies will grow even closer as time moves on. The notion of inclusion is at the forefront of our thinking as educationalists. At present, in the UK, our attention is drawn to gender, race and disability but, as immigration and multiculturalism continue to increase, the nature of UK schools and the values upheld within them will have to evolve. Values based projects in community sports centres already exist across the UK. Football4Unity, run by the University of Brighton, is one excellent example. From my observations of values based coaching and teaching it must be a strong consideration that the PE curriculum continues to evolve alongside the evolving constitution of our society. PE and sport are powerful vehicles for promoting positive human behaviour, increasing its presence and making it a conscious process may become increasingly important as our communities welcome greater diversity.

In a constantly changing society, where we are often sidetracked by obesity levels of children, sedentary teenagers and the small amount of physical activity that pupils are doing, do we sometimes neglect the fundamentals of spiritual, moral, social and humanistic values that the National Curriculum suggests should be embedded in the delivery of physical education? F4P provides an alternative focus. The messages it sends out do not necessarily have to replace other vital functions of physical education but can operate alongside them by simply applying some of the strategies promoted within the F4P manual and brought to life over 5 years of co-existence coaching in Israel.

Notes

1   Additional material for this Chapter was provided by James Wallis.

2   Dorothy Stringer High School, Brighton, is a comprehensive 11–16 school with specialist sport college status.

3   It is planned that by 2008 there will be 350 specialist sports colleges in the UK.

Chapter 10

A VIEW FROM THE ISRAELI SPORTS AUTHORITY

Ghazi Nujidat

During the year 2002 I was invited to a meeting in the main office of the Israeli Sports Authority (ISA) in Tel Aviv; also invited were Caron Sethill and Jane Shurush, both from the British Council in Israel. The aim of the meeting was to look for co-operation in sport-related projects between the Israeli Sports Authority and the British Council. We talked about several ideas and agreed to be in contact in the future. This was the first time I had heard about the British Council's wish to contribute to promoting conflict resolution and co-existence in our complex and fractured society.

A few months later I received another phone call from Jane Shurush, manager of the office of the British Council in Nazareth — the largest Arab town in north Israel. She requested a meeting to discuss the possibility of the Israeli Sports Authority becoming involved in a football project which was to be held in the summer in the north of srael between Arab communities from one side and Jewish communities from the other. She explained that the project, which was called Football for Peace, had begun two years earlier in one community only, had grown to embrace a partnership among three Jewish and three Arab towns and villages. The focus and main attraction of the project was provided by a team of volunteer coaches and leaders from UK universities, led by the University of Brighton. Jane felt that while the British Council had good links with the UK team and a certain level of grassroots community involvement in Israel, the Sports Authority were in a better position to work with local sport organizations.

We had the meeting and we agreed the role that every party would play in the project and we began working together for the next phase of the project which was going to be held in the summer of 2003. In the budget, from monies provided through the ISA, the British Council and other UK sources, we had enough to support the involvement of eight communities operating at four different centres. One of the main challenges was to recruit pairs of Arab and Jewish communities that were committed to the broad aims and objectives of the overall project, namely: peaceful co-existence. To achieve this, what was needed was to go to the communities and suggest their participation in the project. In doing so, we had to explain the concepts and motives behind the project, from one side having a fun-filled football summer camp with coaches from England while at the same time, and most importantly, teaching basic values to our children and providing important opportunities for meetings between Arab and Jewish children.

You might think that this is simple enough given that we are all living in the state of Israel and are likely to be doing so for the foreseeable future, but it is so frustrating and confusing when your country is so fractured. The Israeli population contains a large majority of Jewish citizens, and a smaller but nonetheless significant minority population of Arab and Druze. Within these larger groups there are numerous other religious and political factions. For reasons alluded to in the introduction to this book, relations among all of these groups, particularly between the Jews and the Arabs are characteristically hostile.

In this complex and volatile mixture it is important to find a way for understanding, tolerance and co-operation between all sections of the community. It is not an exaggeration to say that even though often there is only a few miles distance between both Arab and Jewish communities, they only hear about each other in the news on radio and television. The distance is short but the ignorance and misunderstanding is huge between both populations.

The idea of the British Council to concentrate on the relationship between the two populations — the Arab and the Jewish — within Israel itself was wise. Talking grandly about peace and reconciliation between Israel and the Palestinian Authority does little to resolve the problems faced on a daily basis by people inside Israel who still ignore the culture or even the existence of each other. This is not perhaps the main or most obvious place to begin to search for peace in the Middle-East, but it is one very important piece in a very complex jigsaw puzzle.

In my view, this amazing act sets the British Council apart from other associations who are trying to deal with issues of peace and co-existence mostly through dealing with cross-border populations from Israel and the Palestinian Authority or Jordan. While not ignoring the bigger picture, the British Council have seen the benefits of working with the internal population and we in the Sports Authority appreciate this initiative and are willing to work in full co-operation without any hesitation.

The Sports Authority in Israel is a Department in the Ministry of Education, Culture and Sport, and is responsible for all the sport in Israel whether it is public sport or competitive/private sport. The Sports Authority is also responsible for developing the sport facilities and sport teams in all Israel regardless of whether Arab or Jewish. In this respect we are encouraging special initiatives in sports, particularly in the north of Israel where we have the biggest concentration of Arab and Jewish populations. We define such initiatives as sport for coexistence and we have several of these projects such as horse riding, contemporary and ethnic dancing, even children marching for peace and young people riding together for reconciliation. As of today, however, our main project has become Football for Peace because it has proven to be both attractive and accessible to children from both community traditions.

It was natural that we would work together with the British Council and the Brighton University staff on all the details which concern the project. There was a clear role for every partner. From our side the Sports Authority, in consultation with the British Council, dealt with questions concerned with which communities would take part in the project, the resource allocation for each community, the recruitment of local training staff to work alongside UK volunteers, and the level of co-operation and key contacts in the local councils or municipalities. In order to achieve these objectives, first we (the regional Sport Supervisors) listed the names of the Arab and the Jewish communities in the Galilee which were closest to each other. To be short-listed, another criterion for the selection of communities was concerned with the quality of available facilities and, most importantly, the existence of a decent sized grass playing area. A record of financial stability and good resource management was a third criterion; and, finally but nonetheless significant, the level of enthusiasm for the project and its aims from the local Sport Director was an important deciding factor.

Once the short-list of communities had been drawn up another meeting with the British Council was held to discuss the candidates and determine the final pairings. Each step of this process was communicated to the key staff at the University of Brighton, two of whom visited Israel in December preceding the project and, together with the local staff from the Sports Authority and the British Council, visited every venue to have a direct and real picture about all the prevailing conditions. Only after this inspection visit was a final decision taken whether or not the community would be invited to participate in the project. If a community was rejected, they were given a clear idea of why and invited to apply again in the future once they had been able to fulfil the conditions outlined above.

Experience suggested to us that we needed to have clear and formal agreements about what was to be provided for each community by the ISA and what they were expected to provide in return to facilitate the smooth running of the project in their towns and villages. Each of the selected communities were sent a letter congratulating them on their acceptance into the programme and outlining in detail what their grant for the project would be and what they were required to provide. For their part, each community was required to provide a signed letter of commitment from the mayor of the council agreeing to accept all the conditions for having a successful project. We felt that it would be important to show our UK guests at least a small sample of traditional culture and hospitality from both an Arab and a Jewish perspective. With this in mind we agreed that each community had to host the whole UK team during their visit for some traditional hospitality, for a tour and a communal meal.

Once the eight participating communities were established they were required to nominate someone of stature and responsibility to join with representatives from the BC and the ISA to form a project planning group. This had obvious advantages in terms of ironing out the practical logistics of the whole programme and the details of each community's particular needs. It also had the added advantages of bringing into contact senior sport leaders from neighbouring communities who, in the normal course of events, would not routinely work together. The first task for this planning group was to agree among themselves and with the University of Brighton leaders the most appropriate dates for the project. This was not easy — in Israel having to take account of school term times and holidays, and the different religious holidays and festivals in the Jewish, Islamic and Christian calendars, and in the UK having to consider University terms, examination schedules and graduation ceremonies. Eventually, it was agreed that the best time to run the project was during the first two weeks of July.

While the UK student volunteer coaches were to lead the F4P coaching sessions, they would be assisted by young, local volunteer coaches to be recruited, pro-rata, from the participating communities. The local coaches were required to have a basic ability in English language and each UK coach would be assigned one Arab and one Jewish coach. There were three reasons for this: firstly, they could be of practical assistance in helping with the coaching sessions; secondly, they could help with translation; and finally, they would provide another layer of contact across otherwise divided communities.

In order to inculcate these volunteers with the practices and philosophies underpinning F4P and to integrate them with the UK volunteer coaches with whom they would be working, we decided to organize a training day to take place the day before the project-proper started in the communities. We began looking for a suitable venue for the training day. Several places were suggested and we had to decide which was the best place, according to the level of the facilities, the price, availability, the distance from the communities, and security. We choose the Hagoshreem Kibbutz Hotel close to the border with Lebanon. Even then (before the renewed cross-border conflict of July 2006) we were aware of the security situation along the northern border between Israel and Lebanon. But, mercifully, 2002–2003, a time when Israeli forces had withdrawn completely from Lebanese territory, was a relatively peaceful period and we decided to take the risk and choose this lovely place.

At this point in the project's development, all of the UK team stayed in a central location and travelled in rented cars in groups of five each day to the communities in which they would be working. The next step for the planning team was to find a suitable place for the accommodation of the UK group. As well as being somewhere affordable within our slender budget, this had to be in a central place from where it would be easy to reach the several coaching venues. An unfortunate by-product of the escalation in conflict in Israel and Palestine since 2000 has been the collapse of the tourism industry. Because of its biblical associations and revered Christian history, the Galilee — or the Holy Land, as it is often referred to in Christian circles — has a well developed tourist infrastructure which because of the conflict was drastically under capacity. We were able to take advantage of this and book a good and relatively cheap hotel in Nazareth, in the heart of the region in which all of our project sites were located.

Once the planning concerned with the five days of coaching that would take place in the communities had been taken care of, our next task was to select a venue to host the final football festival and tournament. One of participating communities was Afula, a largely Jewish market town about 30kms away from Nazareth. They had a large facility that was deemed to be sufficient for this event and they initially offered to let us use it. However, only a matter of weeks before the commencement of project, Afula withdrew this offer, claiming that there were problems over insurance. Hurriedly we used our relations with neighbouring sport departments and we found a venue in Kfar Tavor, another Jewish community at the foot of Mount Tabor, a sacred Christian site where the Transfiguration of Christ was reputed to have taken place. The stadium at Tavor was large enough, but the playing surface was in poor condition and on the day of the finals the sun beat down relentlessly, with the temperature soaring to around 100 degrees. Nonetheless, in keeping with an ethos that was to become typical of F4P, the coaches shrugged their shoulders in the face of adversity and got on with the job of turning the event into a great success. At the end of the football, the British Ambassador to Israel, His Excellency Sherard Cowper-Coles, presented each child with a medal and the winning teams with trophies before hosting a communal meal for VIP guests and all of the F4P staff.

This had been the Sports Authority's first involvement with F4P and for us it was a very important experience. Our role until that time had been just to encourage communities from both sectors Arab and Jewish to take part in the project, and try to help to overcome as much as possible the difficulties encountered on the way. However we had seen and experienced enough to realise that F4P was a serious project that we could use to help to realise some of our own ambitions with regard to using sport as a vehicle to overcome prejudice and bring young people together.

Even at the beginning we notice that we are dealing with a professional staff knowing exactly what they want to do and why. More than this they know how to achieve their objectives, even though they don't hesitate asking for advice from others, especially from the locals in issues concerning interactions with the local population. This appreciation of and respect for local customs and traditions and sensitivity to and openness towards local feelings and opinions is one of the main things which contributed to the respect that the local partners gained for the UK staff, especially Brighton University and the British Council. After the 2003 project we had a feedback meeting with the UK coaching team and all of the participating partners, taking note of the good things that happened and the not so good, and committing ourselves to a bigger and improved project the following year.

In the following weeks, the phone lines between the British Council and the Sports Authority began to be hot as we started looking towards the next year. Making our calculations, from all aspects financially and logistically, we agreed that we could expand from eight to twelve communities. We sent letters to all the sports departments in the north of Israel and more communities showed interest in joining the project. One of the key obser-vations to emerge from the preceding evaluation meeting was that there were too many local volunteers who had been involved who did not fully appreciate the purpose and practices of F4P. Then, in December 2003, Jane Shurush came with a very important suggestion about the possibility of sending a delegation from the communities which would be participating in the project in 2004 to England for one week to undergo training in F4P's ethos and method. I think it was a remarkable idea which moved the project several degrees higher.

The British Council and the Sports Authority began to determine the criteria for the selection of participants in this delegation. At first, one con-dition was that only those under the age of 25 could participate in the dele-gation. This proved to be unworkable because we needed to get the most experienced and influential community leaders on board, and these were all over the age of 25. I thought that if I came with this idea to send young trainees to England instead of them, surely they would not be so enthusiastic to support the project. So my idea, which I explained to the British Council and to the Brighton staff, was that because this was to be the first delegation concerning the project to visit the UK and our main partners are the local Sport Directors, it would be worth taking them and a person that they would select as the main F4P project coordinator for their communities as representatives. Obviously, being older, many of those selected would not be contributing much in terms of hands-on football coaching, but they could set up training programmes once they returned to their towns and villages. What would be lost in terms of this practical input would be more than made up for from the political advantage of bringing this calibre of person to the UK training event. In the end my idea was accepted, and we moved farther toward the final preparations for the visit to the UK which was scheduled to take place in March 2004.

We finalised a group of 28 members, including myself from the Sports Authority and Jane Shurush from the British Council's Israel office. After a final meeting in Nazareth to confirm important details, we flew to England, arriving in London in the evening, and from there we travelled to Eastbourne on the south coast where the University of Brighton's Department specialising in sports is located (Chelsea School). We were put up in a pleasant hotel overlooking the seafront, only a relatively short walk from the University campus. The training programme consisted of a day of ice-breaking outdoor activities (team problem solving, orienteering, raft building etc.) followed by three days of F4P-style football coaching alongside UK volunteers and with local school children. All of this activity was liberally interspersed with lectures, meetings, films and social activities. A highlight of the visit came at the end with a day trip to London, culminating in an escorted tour of the then English Premiership Champions Arsenal's Highbury stadium before departing for the airport and a late night flight back to Tel Aviv.

For the Israeli group it was a wonderful experience, and the feedback that we got from those who participated was very encouraging. They were so amazed by the commitment of the UK team, whether they were the management staff or the students. The entire programme had been prepared down to the smallest detail and the variety of the activities was very good and more than fulfilled our expectations. The group had to be active in a very intensive way, and even though many of them were past their physical best, they showed high motivation to do all the challenges that we had to face during our stay in England. They gained many educational manners and values in a short period of time and they were astonished by the UK professionalism in so many things. They particularly admired the inventive ways through which the training programme led the Israeli group to get close to each other, helping them to leave the barriers and negative interpersonal attitudes behind them. Much of the feedback was about how strong the impact of the travel and training week had been on the members of the delegation, whether they are Arabs or Jewish, and how strange it was that all the time they were abroad they had all acted as Israeli without the title Arab or Jewish, even at times joking with one another about the situation back home! By the time of their departure they felt that they had been trained to come back to Israel and deliver all these things to the children in their home communities, enabling them to contribute to pushing the train of the coexistence a short distance farther.

It was a very important study tour which produced the exact results that we wanted. As hoped, the most important thing that we got from the members of the Israeli delegation was a full commitment to the success of the project in July 2004. With the full commitment of the Sports Directors and the coordinators of the communities we were able to move forward much more easily and have all of our requirements for the preparation of the project fulfilled.

As with the previous year we planned to have a training day when the UK team arrived and before the commencement of coaching in the communities. For the training day, we had asked about the possibility of having it the National Israeli Sports University, Wingate. Because this institution is connected to the Sports Authority we were able to book its extensive facilities and use Wingate's residential facilities for the UK team. On Friday morning July 2, 2004 the U.K. group arrived in Israel and on Saturday we had a very successful training day at Wingate. This left the team well prepared to begin coaching in the 13 communities (7 Arab and 6 Jewish) the following day. At the end of the week the final tournament was held in the modern stadium of Nazareth — a 5,000 capacity stadium with extensive training pitches. At the end of the tournament it was an unforgettable picture seeing more than 700 girls and boys in a huge celebration, without a difference between Arab or Jewish children.

The day after the tournament we had a feedback session which yielded important views for improving the project: from one side to increase the number of the communities participating in the project; and from the other side to keep the high standard and quality of the coaching/playing while at the same time maintaining the ethos and co-operative values that underpin the programme.

After the evaluation and feedback meeting, the UK group travelled to the south for two days. This was for relaxation and compensation for the hard work done by the volunteers during the week. It was my job to suggest the program to the British Council so I looked for something different from what the group would be used to back home, whether it is the weather or the way of living. With this in mind I proposed making a tour to the south of Israel to the Negev Desert to be hosted in a Bedouin camp, riding camels, learning Bedouin tracking methods, and enjoying traditional Bedouin hospitality before spending the night in communal Bedouin tents. After the Negev, the group spent a day and a night at a Dead Sea resort hotel before returning to Tel Aviv and flying home. This brief period of rest and relaxation was well deserved and much appreciated by the UK team.

As we looked to extend the scope of the project for 2005, one of the major problems we were faced with was to do with resources. As the numbers of project partner communities grew (2005 n=19) an already slender budget remained static and we needed to look for ways to save money. It was quite expensive to accommodate all of the UK team in a central hotel and rent several cars to transport them to the various project sites. We floated the idea of having each pair of communities take responsibility for hosting the UK coaching team that was to be responsible for their particular project for the duration of the event. This would mean that four coaches and one leader would need to be billeted together, fed and watered and transported to and from the coaching venues. This idea was accepted, albeit reluctantly at first, by the leaders of the UK team. As it turned out, this proved to be a most successful innovation as it allowed the UK volunteers to get much closer to the communities with which they were working and get to know their hosts — their customs, traditions, ways of life— more intimately. Some of the volunteers in 2005 had been with F4P in previous years when accommodation had been in a central hotel and they were unequivocal in their support for these more localised hosting arrangements.

Until 2005 we had been working with largely rural based towns and villages that were either exclusively Jewish or exclusively Arab. Another new idea which was implemented in the project of 2005 was having an urban community with Jewish and Arab districts. In the north we have few 'mixed' communities such as the coastal ports of Haifa and Akko. We chose the town of Akko as a pilot for having the project in an urban environment because it is smaller and suffers from greater neglect. The 'mixed' towns in Israel are typified by tension between the Arab and the Jewish populations, fed not just by political differences but also by social and economic inequality. The Arab minority in 'mixed' towns suffer from bad conditions. Mostly they live in old slums, struggling to get better conditions in education, homes and jobs. Most of them live below the level of poverty. On the other side you have the Jewish population where many live well above the level of poverty, enjoying much better living conditions. The same is true of the smaller rural towns and villages, but because they are exclusively one or the other, the discrepancies in the quality of life are not so readily apparent. So when you want to make a common activity, such as Football for Peace, you will see that all these problems will show themselves in a place like Akko. You will notice the keeping of distance between the two peoples which not all of the time will be between Arab and Jewish. Some time you will notice the solidarity between Arab and Jewish people from poor and old slums from one side in the face of the Jewish people who come from modern, well-off and stable neighbourhoods.

In 2005 we mounted the most successful F4P ever, with 19 communities participating in eight separate projects and all taking part in a very successful tournament, hosted in the town of Um al Fahem and honoured by a visit from senior representatives from The FA of England. As is to be expected, once the project was over we had our collective evaluation meeting which reached overwhelmingly positive conclusions. There were, however, some issues that had to be aired and ironed out and these are explored below.

The official attitude of the Ministry of Education and Sports is to encourage participation in any kind of educational sporting activity and they are also budgeting for such projects. However, when you come to the communities with suggestions for such activities, we face a strange phenomenon. In the Arab communities we get a direct and positive answer of accepting the challenge and being ready to give any assistance needed for the success of the project. I feel sorry to admit that we face a few frustrations when dealing with some of the Jewish communities. In the beginning both sides show enthusiasm and commitment to the idea which underpins the project and they appreciate what the staff from the UK are trying to do to improve our children's way of thinking and their attitudes toward each other. But later we begin to detect some hesitations and questions, and mostly these questions come from the Jewish partners, like ' how much budget are we going to get and is the budget going to cover all the expenses?'; or 'it's going to be hard recruiting children in July, because most of the children will be in a summer camps or in a vacations with the parents'; or 'the sports facilities will not be available'; or 'it's going to be hard finding enough local young trainers'. Sometimes they don't hesitate to cancel their participation in the project even if you have done all the arrangements with them and it is only a few weeks until the start of the project. For instance, this is what happened with the Jewish town of Afula in 2004 when they had been part of the project throughout all of the arrangements, including sending two representatives to the training week in England. One month before the beginning of the project the Sports Director phoned our office to tell us that they had problems with the trainers and recruitment of children, and it was too short notice to find other volunteer coaches, so they were canceling their participation in the project. This is just one of many examples.

So we ask the natural question, why this difference between words and actions? In reality it seemed to be that the minority Arab population is more eager for reconciliation and understanding rather than the majority. All the time we are getting applications and requests from Arab communities to be part of the project. Also, a pattern has emerged whereby, even when they do stay committed at a municipal level, the Jewish communities often find it difficult to get enough children to join the project and balance out the numbers of Arab children who flock to take part.

We may speculate as to some of the factors that might contribute to this asymmetric response to F4P:

— For security reasons, Jewish parents are worried about sending their children to Arab communities;

—Many of the Jewish communities charge money for participating in the project which puts poorer children off.

— Unlike their Arab counterparts, Jewish children have a variety of activities to join in the summer (such as summer activity camps) rather than being in a football field.

—Arab communities suffer from a lack of sports facilities and summer programs, so when F4P is given without charge, the parents prefer sending them to the project.

One of the important requirements for the success of the project is a professional and committed coordinator who can give immediate answers, and promote good relations with the community and with the officials. Coexistence is a good slogan but when you need to dig inside and try to make things happen, you prefer that others deal with it rather than you. The Jewish Sports Department has a variety of sports activities throughout the year, so the Sports Director avoids another burden in the summer when he feels the need of a vacation or works privately in the summer camps. The same thing can be said of some of the Arab Sports Directors, although the Arab Sport Directors find in such an activity an opportunity to come and show their enthusiasm for and expertise in sports with involvement of foreign partners. This is something which can help them in increasing the budget for the Sport Department from the mayor of the council.

The prevailing climate of conflict means that still there are social pressures and political influences on the attitudes of both sides towards each other, and you find hesitation and mutual suspicion from both sides. It is not easy to counteract the ignorance between two populations and try to build trust between both sides after being exposed so long to aggressive and hostel attitudes. Certainly, it is more attractive for the children to participate in an activity when foreign trainers are involved rather than local trainers, and for the organisers the idea of having the one week study in England gives the project superiority over other projects. Also, the UK partners keep neutral in any issue connected to the conflict between Jewish and Arab people and by doing so, in a wise way, they are accepted and welcomed by both populations.

Another issue we have to face is that in most Arab communities there are severe financial problems, so it is not so easy for the Sport Directors to persuade the council officials to support the project. There have been cases when they do not use the budget that we (the ISA) give for the project but spend it on other things. So we find other, creative solutions to be sure that our financial support is used for the intended purposes. One such strategy involved Jewish and Arab partner communities wherein the Sport Director from the Arab community was worried that ISA money meant for F4P might be misdirected by other local officials. To safeguard these resources, he asked us to deliver all of the budget to the Sport Director of the Jewish community (whom he may have befriended during his trip to England), so he could take care of all the expenses needed for both communities!

For all of these reasons and more, we in the Sports Authority are more committed to F4P than any other educational sportive project which deals with multi culture interconnections and mutual understanding. The Sports Authority is investing a big budget in the Football for Peace project, and this reflects the priority we assign to its success in this project. After three years of partnership between the Sports Authority and the British Council and the Brighton University we feel fortunate to be part of a professional staff and feel the satisfaction of contributing to the future generation in delivering basic human manners and building a healthy and peaceful society.

These limitations are far outweighed by F4P's achievements. Just to be there and hear Jewish parents so happy when their child comes home and speaks to them so gladly about an Arab boy whom he met in the project, and they are so good, and he is waiting for tomorrow to meet them. Seeing the faces of these parents, expressing quiet gladness, gives us the energy and determination to continue with our partners in this important project. All participating communities have a strong feeling of gratitude and admiration to the UK partners, particularly University of Brighton and the British Council, and this is reflected in the generous hospitality that the communities arrange for the UK group during their visits to Israel.

Another thing we insist upon is an ongoing programme for the local partners to have a monthly common activity, in any kind of sports or social activity. For us the important thing is the meeting and keeping up the relations between the children and their parents established through F4P. With a few communities this works very well, with others it is more difficult. In the future this will be one of the conditions for communities to continue to be member of the Football for Peace project.

Hopefully, this ongoing programme of cross-community activity will help to make the short-term achievements of F4P more sustainable and lead to the development of more robust structures for coexistence. For those communities already involved in the project, F4P is part of their calendar as a main activity of the Sport Department. What we wish for the future is that we get to a point that this project or something with the same motives of this project will become a natural part of every Sport Department in every municipality in Israel. Only when we reach this point will we know that our work is finished.

On a personal note, being involved in such a noble project is a big honour. I feel privileged to be working with all the professional staff in both Brighton University and the British Council staff. Their commitment and professionalism is remarkable and is a shining light for the dark days that normally characterise the relations between Arab and Jewish populations. As one who grew up close to nature[1] and who knows the changes of the seasons of the year, we have to prepare for the future generation a new spring with optimistic principals and help them to raise green fields covered with roses and brightness. Only through this can we fulfil our term in life in a productive way. For me this is what the Football for Peace symbolises. I will be committed to such a project or anything like it, and try to make my contribution in confirming strong roots for reconciliation and understanding within my country and among my people. Maybe the children who have experienced F4P will not grow up to be professional football players, but surely they will be better human citizens because of it.

Note

[1] Ghazi is a Bedouin Arab.

Chapter 11

THE NEUTRAL LENS: CONSTRUCTING A VISUAL CRITIQUE OF FOOTBALL FOR PEACE

John Doyle

Introduction

During its existence Football for Peace has been the subject of numerous research activities which attempt to understand the impact of the project on individuals. This research also attempts to understand the nature of the project itself and its many meanings for those who experience it. Initial attempts to gather research data primarily utilised questionnaires translated into both Hebrew and Arabic to measure the coaches and children's attitudes before and after engagement with the project. The researchers also conducted numerous interviews with key personnel and participants. All research data was translated into English and the results have led the project leaders to claim that, in the short to medium term, participation in the project can have a positive impact on children's and coaches perceptions of the 'other' community (Stidder and Sugden: p. 138). Moreover the researchers claim this indicates that F4P is not only a valuable vehicle through which children can begin to think about co-existence and mutual understanding, but it is also an important vehicle for changing the way community leaders and policy makers think about how sport can be utilized as a cross-community resource (Lambert, *et al.* 2004b).

But such traditional methods of data collection may be inadequate to uncover the more subtle meanings and understandings of the project. In order to capture the range of experiences during a long term involvement in the project, the diverse perspectives created by engagement in Football for

Peace and the fluctuating ideological standpoints of individuals who engage with the project, the research team has experimented with different methodological tools. This methodological expansion has involved an increasing use of visual media. The development of these methods has reflected changes in the nature of the project which have allowed the research methods and strategies to be adapted and refined. Two digital film projects have complemented this methodological shift. In 2004 the project leaders employed an Israeli film crew to document the project, a decision that proved to be problematic, with difficulties arising due to the film crew's clumsy interventions and intrusions into the project. In 2005 a German documentary film-maker also made a documentary film, 'Children of the Jordan Valley', which focused on one of the projects in which a German student volunteer coach worked.

Alongside these external film productions I have been engaged in filming key features of the project. Field research using this new methodological framework has now run the length of two projects and has yielded a range of data from diverse vantage points. Both the research data and the actual process of research have heightened awareness of many of the ambiguities which the project attempts to navigate and has also posed difficult questions about the project. The research has also been able to provide insights into the success of the project and its worth as an intervention into an alien environment and complex cultural milieu.

I will now go on to describe some of the methodological influences on this research, outline the process of my own research and reflect on some of the different types of field experiences. I will also focus in detail on two separate events during my field work that may offer some insight into some of the strengths and weaknesses of using these methodologies and adapting them for research purposes. Finally I will begin to locate this research project within a theoretical tradition, highlight some of the wider issues that the research has raised and assess the impact the methodology has had on my understanding of the project.

The development of a visual research strategy

There has been a recent expansion of the use of visual methodologies within the social sciences, primarily driven by the availability of cheap and user-friendly technology. Writing about visual research, John Berger (1977: p. 7) stated that "seeing comes before words ... and establishes our place in the surrounding world". In the western imagination, the visual predominates and we are now in an age of what some commentators have called the 'hyper-visual'. Social science researchers have always employed visual means of collecting and recording data, many of the earliest sociological and anthropological studies were supported with visual material. However, a number of researchers have attempted to utilise visual methods alone in attempting to analyse, interpret and transform the social world.

Photography's tradition as a tool for researching social life has primarily reflected a realist conception of the social world. Researchers such as Bateson and Mead and Howard Becker pioneered the use of a new research aesthetic and cemented the methodology as a different way of seeing and interpreting the social world. The use of film within social research mirrors this development. Social research methods and 'realist' film making both appear from the same ideological roots and are "founded upon the western need to explore, document, explain, understand, and hence symbolically control the world. It has been what 'we' do to 'them'" (Ruby, 2005: p. 41).

Research filmmakers working in this tradition believe that the camera does not lie but produces reliable and 'objective' data. Such assumptions about the use of the camera in research may be valid from the positivist/empiricist tradition as these filmmakers are concerned with discovering ways of objectively recording data. However Ruby contends that faith in this method of camera use "produces the same dilemma as its print equivalent: it leaves no room for the producer, the process or the audience" (Ruby, 2000: p.177).

Jean Rouch, the French anthropologist and filmmaker, was pivotal in the development of a more 'reflexive' film style. This type of film is concerned with revealing the "created, structured articulations of the film-maker and not authentic, truthful objective records" (Ruby, 2005: p. 44). Rouch's film *Chronicle of a Summer* was in Ruby's view the first consciously reflexive social science film and positioned Rouch as the antithesis of the traditional positivist filmmaker. Film-makers who attempt to work reflexively make films that recognise that 'objectivity' is problematic due to a myriad of subjective truths, the range of power inequities and the creative imperative. Films made in this tradition offer the subjective constructions of both the film-makers and the subjects of the film.

Reflexive research films can also suggest future possibilities for the research data and enable scholars to use the original research materials in ways not imagined by their original producers. One such film-maker was Tim Asch who explored the nature of collaboration between researchers and filmmakers and sought to develop a method that resulted in researchable footage that can be edited, combined sequentially into a narrative and merged observational-style with interpretive reflexivity (Ruby, 2000: p. 115). All research film work was made possible due to technological advances and the availability of portable sound, lightweight cameras and tape recorders. These researchers and film-makers worked in ways that revolutionized the social sciences, non-fiction and even fiction film. The digital revolution now offers some of the conditions that may allow new techniques to unearth further insights into the social world.

Methodology and experience

My experience of using visual research methods began in April 2005 while working as a research assistant at the University of Brighton. I was asked to use digital video to document the Football for Peace project and to collect film data for use for 'research purposes'. At this point my brief was fluid and the data was to be collected in a 'grounded theoretical' way, building the data as I filmed the project. This field research experience was initiated because it coincided with the Israeli coaches, UK coaches and project leaders four day training week in the UK. My role was to film this event, and I had four main goals.

1. To visually document the training week for future analysis.
2. To create promotional material for the project.
3. To capture orchestrated sequences for the creation of a digital video version of the F4P coaching manual.
4. To gain experience using the equipment and get familiar with the research subjects.

This initial field experience was problematic largely because these goals were ambitious and potentially in conflict with one another. I also lacked the technical expertise. One of my first lessons undertaking research of this kind was that documenting the entire project from an overarching 'godlike' perspective is technically and logistically impossible, inherently reactionary and often tells us more about the researchers than the research subjects. I quickly learnt that it is much more productive to focus on a single goal during each field experience.

However my attempts at filming long sequences of football action did allow me to become familiar with the technical aspects of the camera, the skill of following the action and most crucially to become recognisable to the research subjects. The more access I achieved the more I became to the coaches, 'John the camera man'. Also the inevitability of my presence, a ghostly figure in the background, hiding behind a camera, legitimised my involvement on the project and secured a relationship with the coaches which would later become useful.

The goals of capturing promotional photographs or orchestrated film sequences for promotional purposes impacted on the research dimensions of my wide brief. This in turn affected my mastery of the equipment due to the constant switching between the technical and aesthetic conventions of photography and film, which caused the production and processes of both to be disrupted.

The wide brief also jeopardised my research 'persona' as I occasionally sought to orchestrate a sequence or a photograph which was not popular with the coaches. This also impacted on my research in more subtle ways as I was engaging with the project through the promotional domain, i.e. finding the stories and pictures to promote the project, and also as a researcher 'objectively' recording the project and its participants to collect data.

The lack of focus impacted on the promotional material. The production of a series of professional packages would mean the 'staging' of football sequences which is impossible when filming 'off the hoof' for research purposes. This inevitably highlighted the tensions between commercial and research film-making. While not wholly unsuccessful, filming the four days of the training week with these numerous outcomes was too much to expect from one researcher, let alone an inexperienced and novice filmmaker.

With this chastening experience behind me, I hoped that the trip to Israel in July 2005 would allow me to narrow my focus and to channel my research efforts onto one of the eight projects Football for Peace were running in Northern Israel. My brief during this field trip was refined to capture in detail one project with the Jewish community in Megiddo and the Arab community of Um al Fahem (see Chapter Three). These communities were chosen for research filming for a number of reasons. Firstly the Jewish community in this area had participated in previous projects and was known to members of the research team. The Jewish population this area live mainly on kibbutzim, some situated on disputed land. Megiddo is also close to the site of the biblical Armageddon — a decayed ancient hilltop fortress that acts as a rather clumsy metaphor for the political standoff in the wider region.

The town of Um al Fahem borders the West Bank and is cut off from the Palestinian territories by the semi-completed wall — the so-called 'Green Line' — that divides these two countries. It is a predominantly Moslem town with a reputation within Jewish Israel for being 'radical' and pro-Palestinian. Both the past and present of these towns represent the most polarised of the communities the projects would engage with during the summer of 2005. The finals were also scheduled to take place in Um al Fahem, a town that people from the Jewish community would not usually visit, allowing the project to promote the symbolic possibilities of the power of sport.

I was based on a kibbutz and travelled to the coaching camps in both Um al Fahem and Megiddo to record the coaching sessions. During this time I concentrated on capturing the experiences of the UK coaches and this was the main focus for my research. The actual process of filming this particular project in depth — rather than chasing around the country getting snippets of all of the projects — allowed me to become familiar with the coaches, to begin the process of understanding what they got out of the experience and to assess the impact the project made on them as coaches. The decision to focus research on the UK coaches was made for a number of reasons. I only had one camera, limited time and a wide range of perspectives to gather. There were also language and translation problems to be overcome as well as issues of power relations associated with researching children and people of different cultures to be worked out. I deliberately decided that the collection of research data featuring local children and coaches was to be left for the future when I was better equipped, more technologically able and had more background knowledge of my subjects.

My role as a researcher with a similar cultural background to the other coaches (predominantly male, white, British and Irish graduates) allowed me to be a conduit for them to explain their experiences and their perspectives on the project. However I found it more difficult than in the UK to withdraw into the background with my camera. In Israel, the heat, tense atmosphere and alien environment made my attempts to get close to the coaches more difficult. In fact, initially I was treated with suspicion and hostility by the UK coaches — one coach deliberately kicked the ball at me while I was filming at my tripod. The numerous comments about my presence gradually gave way to grudging acceptance, then to accommodation and finally to co-operation. This allowed me to fade into the background with the tacit support and acceptance of the coaches. This acceptance was then reciprocated by the Israeli coaches and children who, though second on my list of research priorities for this trip were still needed as the source of research material and I wanted to begin the process of relationship building for the future.

The most difficult issue I found using digital video as a data collection tool during this field trip was gaining consent and constant access to the research subjects. One event which highlights how these issues can impact on research was when my presence with the camera was rejected by the project leaders and coaches. This caused difficulty for me collecting data but paradoxically opened up other opportunities.

The issue that caused these difficulties was the community of Um al Fahem's refusal to let the girl's project share facilities with the boy's projects on the finals day. This decision made during the week in Israel was in opposition to the principles that Football for Peace was trying to promote, particularly with regard to 'equity and inclusion'. This event was caused indirectly by the choice of stadium for the final, the use of untested local partners and the lack of understanding by some on the project of how external events and local customs and traditions can impact on the project's 'principals and values' (see Chapter Seven).

This issue caused a major problem with some of the coaching staff who objected to the fracturing of the F4P 'values'. This dispute came to a head during a social event one evening with discussions getting heated as the project leaders dealt with how to manage this blow in a fair and transparent way. However my working relationships with the project leaders and coaches meant that I felt unable to film these arguments due to the sensitivity of the issues to individuals and the wider project. Given that I had chosen to use film as my research methodology, my scribbles into my notebook now seemed inadequate and I felt unable to capture a defining moment of the project. My unease was confirmed when I plucked up the courage to approach the periphery of the huddles of conversation and was left in no doubt that I was unwelcome with my camera and should not film these discussions.

This issue raises important questions of the possibilities of remaining 'objective' and also about my use of film as a methodology for capturing the whole social scene around the project. However an important breakthrough left me feeling that perhaps my presence was not required at this moment and more sensitive, ethical and rigorous ways of getting the same data can be utilised. A couple of the female coaches involved in the dispute recorded video diaries that explicitly explained their viewpoint of this issue and their un-mediated perspective. Having access to this film allowed me access to data and perspectives that I would never have been able to obtain myself, data that was more clearly expressed than the garbled arguments of the night in question. This event also confirmed my emerging view that to adequately represent all the viewpoints on this project the final research films needed to be a shared research exercise with different vantage points being covered by different cameras, uncovering a range of perspectives and allowing access to all areas of the Football for Peace 'experience'.

A new research plan

During this field work I did talk and interact with Israeli coaches and children and these interactions confirmed my intention to deal with these respondents in a different way. Like the issue with the female coaches outlined above, issues of the representation of gender, race and class were so evident as my involvement as a researcher grew, that I knew I would be unable to adequately present these experiences in a way that was either comfortable to me as an individual or ethically sound as researcher. These experiences led me to formulate a research design for the next phase of the data collection in 2006.This design had to take into account that filming in the same way I did with the UK coaches would render any attempt to understand the project from any of the diverse Israeli perspectives moribund.

Throughout the period of my involvement in the project I had become increasingly concerned about some of its core assumptions and this was beginning to affect the way I thought about carrying out my visual research. The contexts within which Football for Peace works, the compromises the project leaders have to make and the relationships it has to maintain to survive all impact on the usefulness of data produced in this way and the 'neutrality' claims the project makes. Some of the tools that Football for Peace utilises can be seen to be problematic. The coaching manual, devised by British project leaders, comprising of 'principles and values' plucked from a British socio-cultural system, is one such tool.

In addition, some of the project's core partnerships must be critiqued. The project's relationship with what some on the political 'left' view to be a neo-imperialist state body, the British Council, promoting British 'values' to the world through the resurrection of the protean myths of British sport, is one such relationship. The tentative support of an FA increasingly concerned with its international power, prestige and profile is another.

Other local issues such as the involvement and support of the State of Israel via the Israeli Sports Authority and issues around the use of English and Hebrew as working languages on the project also potentially fracture any claims of 'neutrality'. These relationships and the decisions they gener-ate all conspire to ask questions of the project and the motives of those insti-tutions that either offer or decline to support it. More importantly they poten-tially disenfranchise some on the project, threatening the legitimacy of the claim that all voices of those involved on the project are heard and possibly blocking the voices of any discontents within the project. With this in mind I concluded that before the films were to be completed, rushes — draft film footage — should be available via the Football for Peace website for critique and comment, and that Jewish and Arab Israelis should film themselves to offer their perspectives on the project and its wider meanings to them.

In order to achieve the results I wanted and to reflect the full range of experiences, I realised that I needed a research budget and more digital resources than I had been working with. I bid for some research funds and was granted a budget and digital video equipment in kind, in order to carry out this project in more breadth and depth. This injection of resources en-sured the website was developed to accommodate video and host a forum where the films could be discussed, initially in English but also potentially in Hebrew and Arabic. I was also able to purchase five sets of digital equip-ment for field research. These were to be distributed to Israeli coaches and children to film aspects of their lives and their experiences and engagement with the Football for Peace project.

The first field work using this method was initiated in April 2006 when the Israeli coaches arrived for the annual training week in the UK. While I was filming the training programme and interviewing the project leaders, I handed one camera to a small number of Israeli coaches to film the four days they were in the UK, speaking in Hebrew and Arabic so they felt able to adequately describe their experiences in the UK, in their own language. I issued only one camera due to the time involved reviewing and editing the rushes and the potential cost of translation, but it acted as a microcosm of the proposed summer project, to see how well the experiment worked, whether the coaches felt comfortable using the technology and getting involved in this type of research.

The positive feedback from the Israeli coaches suggested the process could overcome some of the issues of context, language, culture and power. With this model in place for the future I looked forward to the July trip to

Israel in order to attempt to get some more nuanced and detailed research data from the diverse Israeli respondents. My revised research plan for July 2006 in Israel during two weeks of research was the following.

1. To film the Israeli preparations for the summer's project in Akko.
2. To distribute the cameras to children and coaches from all communities in Akko.
3. To provide instruction on the technical aspects of the camera equipment and advice on filming.
4. To film the projects in Akko.

Akko was chosen for a number of reasons. Firstly it was a project that had experienced difficulties the previous year and one that saw a new local team take on responsibility for the project. Akko is also one of the most mixed of the communities that was to host Football for Peace, with many communities living side by side in this ancient port city. Akko's history is one of conquest and re-conquest by western and eastern powers going hand in hand with the co-existence of diverse communities. Placed by the UN partition plan of 1947 within a Palestinian state, it was immediately annexed by the state of Israel during the war of 1948. The city appears untypical of Israel with a mixture of communities living side by side. However scratch away at the surface and even in this most laidback of cities the ethnic and religious divisions become clear (see Chapter Four).

Divisions among the established 'black' Arab communities and the light skinned Arabs and European Jews and the more recent immigration of Moroccan and Ethiopian 'black' Jews and Russians add to the local disputes. However the ever present wider conflict between Palestinians and the State of Israel is evident in the sectarian geography of the city. The old town, a ragged maze of ancient streets within the old fortress, is predominantly Arab and Moslem, with newer high rise developments, with mixed communities that act as a buffer to the predominantly European Jewish suburbia that surrounds the old town.

I arrived in Israel four days in advance of the main Football for Peace team in order to film and research the preparations for the Akko project and to meet and familiarise myself with the city, the local coaches and the children. However as soon as I arrived at my accommodation in old town Akko, I was informed of the kidnapping of two Israeli soldiers and the inevitable response by the Israeli Defence Force that would be the initial stages of a war between Israel and Hezbollah in Lebanon. This war continued for a month, cancelling the Football for Peace projects and forcing me to return home (see the Postscript). However one incident on my first night, before the missiles were exchanged, allowed me to witness some of the internal difficulties within Israel at first hand. This incident has led me to question further the value of principals such as 'neutrality' and 'objectivity', and therefore some of the core values and claims of Football for Peace.

My early arrival meant that I was freed from the restrictions of the Football 4 Peace project team and the united face all Israelis generally show to the outside world. On arrival I was immediately taken to an Israeli-Palestinian wedding ceremony, where issues of 'neutrality' and 'objectivity' were immediately brought to the fore. Our contact in Akko — Ibrahim, an Israeli Palestinian coach — took me to his home on an estate of concrete flats, much like any other in any city. I am here to film a 'Henna ceremony' which is a wedding ritual which involves the groom bringing henna to the bride for their wedding henna tattoos.

On a communal piece of wasteland that connects the three main blocks of flats, loud Arabic music blasts from a mobile disco and around forty young Arabic women dance. Surrounding them sit older Arab women in Hajibs and younger children. On the periphery are the Arab men, some barely taking notice, talking amongst themselves, the majority arguing with two policemen who have come to shut down the wedding celebrations. The men become increasingly agitated with the police. I'm suddenly not only recording this but become a social actor as an old woman talks to me in Arabic, Ibrahim translates and tells me she says I should be filming this to record how 'they' — the police — harass 'us' the Arab community.

My immediate thought is to continue recording and walk over to get nearer the action but I am struck with a number of dilemmas. Do I get close enough to film and risk getting my camera broken or confiscated as soon as I have arrived in the field? Does filming a situation like this inflame the scene? Does filming this scene constitute my relinquishing of my 'neutrality' and 'objectivity' as a researcher, given the wider context within which I am working on the project?

I decide to film from afar using my 'night shot', preferring to capture the essence of the dispute rather than placing myself at the centre of the scene. It feels like a compromise of the 'neutral' researcher and the 'objective' recorder of social life against the interventionist activist. Eventually the dispute with the police is calmed and Ibrahim takes me up to his home to film the ceremony from his back window. After ten minutes the ceremony is halted by the police returning to disrupt the celebrations: now the anger of the local community is incandescent.

The police have now arrested one of the male revellers for 'drug dealing' after chasing him through the wedding party. Again I am facing the dilemma of intervening with my camera and becoming part of the social scene or recording from afar.

I am urged repeatedly by more than one woman to continue filming, 'to show what the Jewish are like', and 'how they treat us' as it's translated, and again I resist. I do however make tentative steps towards the now chaotic scenes and film the aftermath; it is now that I begin to understand some of the wider contexts of this scene and some of the political implications of this type of research. As I zoom in on the arrest I notice a large building in the backdrop and realise that it is a police station making up the fourth side in a wider square block which oversees the three blocks of flats where the wedding event takes place. It seems no coincidence that the locals feel under surveillance and wish someone to record what is happening: the geography of their environment means that they are under constant surveillance and, from the evidence of that night, harassment. So I continue filming but now with a critical eye on the wider political reality of Akko that forms the backdrop to the football projects.

One of the strengths of this approach to visual research is aesthetic: no amount of descriptive prose can do justice to this event. The movement, colours, sounds and general vitality of this scene are heightened when captured unmediated; when un-edited research film data remains an exemplary aide memoir or research record. Also, when mediated by the film maker through editing and placed within a wider context, the final film becomes much more than a document of a social scene and a place in time. It can become a critical and political tool.

Issues of neutrality in research

The remainder of my time in Israel saw the security situation deteriorate further and the Football 4 Peace projects cancelled. I was able to complete two of my objectives, recording the preparations for the Akko project and filming some of the social life of the participants in Akko. However the main goals of my field work remain unfinished. I received one hour of film data from the children and coaches on their preparations for the project. The cancellation of the project meant I was unable to receive data on their opinions of the project, life in Akko and perhaps the war itself. I need therefore to revisit this in the future.

However, the war has affected the process of my research in more fundamental ways. Four days with a community that feels under threat — both inside its ancient fortress from the State and from outside its borders due to a ceaseless war — makes the project's principal of 'neutrality' increasingly hard to endorse. Also the effect of the Lebanon war on the Football for Peace project raises questions about the very principles on which the project is based. It could be argued that the Football for Peace principal of 'neutrality' like the principle of 'objectivity' in visual research is based on an outmoded western and imperial premise.

The British claims of 'neutrality' in the wider conflict between Palestinians and the state of Israel also appear to create difficulties due to the legacy of the British mandate and the British government's interventions in the region. The claims that sport can offer a 'neutral' territory for practitioners to work in is also now to be questioned. Therefore the research process is inevitably affected. If the illusions of neutrality and objectivity are punctured, what theoretical model can inform the visual critique of the project?

I have embarked on this research within what some would loosely refer to as being within a 'cultural studies' tradition. Within this tradition the issues of context and the representation of marginal groups in relation to wider society are paramount. I have attempted to allow room for the voices of all on the project to explain the project's meanings and to reflect on what the project means to them. This may be the best means of examining how individuals relate to the project.

However, other theoretical traditions may be best placed to understand the wider political contexts of the project. Perhaps a more fruitful way to critique the project and its relationship to the wider socio-political milieu is through the lens of what some would term a post-modern critique. The issues of power in Israel and the associated manifestations of this power within communities through surveillance, as evidenced by the filming incident in Akko and articulated by thinkers such as Foucault, are possible theoretical traditions to explore.

As my research agenda has shifted to visually critique the Football for Peace project, an examination of this combination of theory and method may be central to this critique. It allows for a multi-layered approach to research which, mirroring the process of film making, takes the 'scripts' of everyday life and layers them with meanings, focuses on different viewpoints and perspectives, deconstructs a myriad of identities and power relationships, while sweeping across the panorama of social life.

Concluding thoughts

The evolving methodologies outlined here have a number of potential limitations and concerns. The most fundamental issue within social and cultural research traditions is that of the ambiguity of most visual material when compared with written or verbal communication. Critics argue that analysis of visual material is subjective, selective and potentially manipulative, with new technologies making this both more easier and more likely.

These same issues can be found when using textual forms of research analysis. Written quotes are selected to illustrate points just as photographs are framed and staged, and video footage filmed and edited. In textual research data the selection, transcription, contextualisation and analysis of recorded conversation removes from text many of the nuances and subtleties of language. Research data collected using visual methods can overcome the ambiguity of the analysis. The un-doctored photograph or unedited video can remain as appendices to any subjective intervention. Becker has said that all forms of social science data collection have to withstand "logical, epistemological and practical arguments that might be brought against them" (Becker, 2004: p. 196). Visual research methods are just another way of gathering research data.

Some critics also argue that issues of authorial control are heightened when using these methods. However the dissemination of the film 'rushes' through the website and the reflexive feedback I hope to receive will allow me to retain control of this process while still allowing the voices of the research subjects to be heard. An analogy that can be used for this research process is the football coach and his team. The coach prepares his team, chooses the tactics and strategy but then leaves the interpretation of the game to the players. Similarly I hope that by allowing the novice film-makers to 'play' with the cameras, they will interpret their own lives but still allow me to retain editorial control, as the coach retains overall control of his team.

No matter how loosely imposed, issues concerning the editorial process are themselves problematic. One recent episode outlines how editorial decisions can impact on the construction of meaning. The recent documentary film about the 2005 project, 'Children of the Jordan Valley' contains an example of how film data can be manipulated and the intervention of the film-maker can change meanings in order to justify an ideological position or heighten the narrative flow. The film concludes with a downbeat ending, twelve months later on, reflecting one of the boys from one project refusing to meet another boy from the 'other' community, despite their playing together and seemingly making friends in the summer. The implication of this denouement is that the project's goal of bringing communities together in a long term project is ultimately flawed and unsuccessful. However the construction of this scene through the editing process hides the fact that the dispute on the screen is nothing of the sort. It in fact concerns the boy being upset about a domestic dispute around mealtimes and if you understand Hebrew you can tell as much from the soundtrack. Therefore the film-maker's interpretation of the project's 'failure' uses flawed 'evidence' to support the premise.

My objection here is not to question whether the success of the F4P football projects can be 'proved' in any 'objective' way through a narrative film, or to dispute the film-maker's intellectual standpoint, but to point out that such subjective editorial decisions can show the absurdity of the film-maker as a 'neutral, objective' recorder of social life. It also offers evidence that complete authorial and editorial control cannot be relied upon to create the 'truth'. The best the film-maker can do is construct an interpretation, and in 'Children of the Jordan Valley' it is a flawed one. In this case, the film-maker wants to sell his film so he is looking for ways to sensationalise his material. Sociologists and ethnographers are under less pressure to manipulate their data to 'get a good story'. Nevertheless, we should be wary of our own ideological positioning before we go into the editing suite.

One way I hope to overcome this problem is by allowing the research respondents to exercise some degree of editorial control through their own camera use, making their own decisions on what and where they film and what aspects of life they choose to reveal. This 'micro' editing will then form part of the wider editorial process whereby editorial decisions can be commented on and discussed via the website. This is one way to reduce the subjective interpretations of the author/film-maker. However, working in this way will inevitably impact on the film's aesthetic and will fracture the narrative flow.

The use of these research methods also allows researchers to engage with the heightened visual literacy of contemporary culture. Issues such as those outlined above are paramount if the research is framed in a realist paradigm seeking to establish 'truths' rather than interpretations. This research project seeks multiple interpretations of research data, from a range of perspectives in recognition that social life is interpreted differently by social groups.

The research methodologies I have employed have developed over a period of time, adapting to changing circumstances in the field environment, my developing expertise and the needs of the project. This fluctuating methodological framework now needs to adapt to the impact on the project of the 2006 war between Israel and Lebanon. All involved in the project come from different ideological positions and engage in the project in different ways, from looking at the project as a political engagement, seeing it terms of 'making a difference' or as an opportunity to play football. Engaging with and reflecting on this range of perspectives was one of the main research goals. While this diversity cannot always be reconciled it is one of the strengths of the project and what makes it such a rich research environment. However the war may have polarised opinions and skewed perspectives to such a degree that it impacts on both the project and the research.

Also, my engagement with the project as a researcher has led me to feel that the concepts of 'neutrality' and 'objectivity' in relation to the conflict in Israel is problematic. The recent war means I will engage with the project using a more interventionist and critical lens and attempt to locate the project in the wider socio-cultural milieu of the conflict. I believe the strengths of these methods are that they are flexible enough to allow the researcher to adapt to field circumstances and changes in perspective. These strengths also extend to the process of research and the values of reflexivity, inclusivity and accessibility. They allow the transparent collection of data, jointly produced by the researcher and research subjects, to reveal what Football for Peace means to all who experience it and how the project relates to and engages with the wider cultural and political contexts of the region.

Acknowledgements

This chapter is based on research that was made possible by generous funding from the Centre for Excellence in Teaching and Learning (CETL), a joint venture by the Universities of Sussex and Brighton, and by funding from LearnHigher.

References

Becker, H. (2004) 'Photography as evidence, photographs as exposition', in Knowles, C. and Sweetman, P. (eds) *Picturing the social landscape: Visual methods and the sociological imagination*. London, Routledge: pp. 193–198.

Berger, J. (1977) *Ways of seeing*. London: Penguin.

Joecker, S. (2006) *Children of the Jordan Valley*. Magic Hour Productions.

Lambert, J., Stidder, G. and Sugden, J. (2004) 'Football for Peace Coaching Manual', University of Brighton, Unpublished.

Lambert, J., Stidder, G. and Sugden J. (2004) 'Football for Peace (F4P) — teaching and playing sport for conflict resolution in the Middle East', *Euronews*, July.

Ruby, J. (2000) *Picturing culture: Explorations of film and anthropology*. Chicago, London, University of Chicago Press.

Ruby, J. (2005) 'The image mirrored: Reflexivity and the documentary film', in Rosenthal, A. and Corner, J. (eds) *New challenges for documentary*, 2nd edition. Manchester and New York: Manchester University Press, pp. 34–48.

Stidder, G. and Sugden, J. (2003) 'Sport and social inclusion across religious and ethnic divisions: A case study of football in Israel', in S. Hayes and G. Stidder (eds) *Equity and inclusion in Physical Education and sport: Contemporary issues for teachers, trainees and practitioners*. London: Routledge: pp. 135–152.

Sugden, J. (2006) 'The challenge of using a values based approach to coaching sport and community relations in multi-cultural settings. The case of Foot-ball for Peace in Israel', *European Journal for Sport and Society* Vol. 3, No. 1: pp. 7–24.

POSTSCRIPT

WAR STOPS PEACE!

John Sugden

Wednesday, July 12, 2006. The British Airways jet banked over Cyprus ready for its slow descent across the South Eastern Mediterranean into Tel Aviv's Ben Gurion International Airport. Football for Peace 2006 was about to begin. The main party of 40+ volunteer coaches and support staff were scheduled to fly out the following day. I was the advance guard, arriving a day early to check final arrangements and visit the stadium in Jerusalem where the F4P football festival was to be held the following week.

I was nervous. Not because of the flight but because of breaking news coming out of Israel that there had been skirmishes between Hezbollah guerrillas and the Israeli Defence Forces (IDF) () along the border between Israel and Lebanon. There had been several fatalities and two Israeli soldiers had been captured by Hezbollah guerrillas. The IDF were already engaged in serious action further south in the Gaza Strip, where there had been a large mobilisation in the wake of the kidnapping of another Israeli soldier by Palestinian militia. The action in Gaza was some distance from the main centre of our operations in Galilee, but the more recent events along the border with Lebanon were much closer and could jeopardise the 2006 enterprise.

Things had not improved while I had been in the air and, by the time I was deposited at my hotel in Jerusalem, Hezbollah had begun responding to Israel's incursion into Lebanon by firing Katushya missiles at towns and villages in Northern Galilee. One of the first places to be hit was the resort town of Nahariya were the UK coaches were to have spent a couple of days

172

enjoying rest and relaxation at the end of the 2006 project. That evening I was supposed to be having a leisurely dinner in a Jerusalem restaurant with Caron Sethill, the Assistant Director of the British Council in Israel, who is one of F4P's biggest supporters. Instead she picked me up at the hotel and we sped North for a hastily convened meeting in a road-side diner just South of Haifa, Israel's third largest city. My heart sank when, as we drove and listened to the radio, it was reported that missiles had struck Haifa. This meant that virtually all of the communities that had been lined up to host F4P projects were well within missile range. I knew then that irrespective of the outcome of our meeting it would be both impossible and irresponsible to allow F4P 2006 to go ahead.

For the six years that F4P had run we had always said that we might one day have to abort the project at the eleventh hour if the security situation demanded it, and now that time had arrived. It was a gloomy meeting as I sat with Jane and Caron from the British Council and Ghazi and Ofer Butan from the Israeli Sports Authority examining our options, but all of us knowing that there was only one course of action to take. Everybody had worked so hard to prepare for this year's event which was to have been the biggest ever: twenty two communities; eleven projects; 1000+ children; a F4P peace convoy; on the way to the finals festival in Jerusalem's Betar stadium which was also to feature a exhibition match between a UK team and a team of TV celebrities. Expectations were huge which meant that the disappointment would be equally big, both for the partner communities and for the UK volunteers.

Even as we talked the main party was gathering at London's Stansted Airport, but I had told the party leaders not to check anybody in until they had heard from me. A decision could not be delayed. We had a duty of care to the children who had signed up to the project and at a time when they and their families had been warned to either stay in or close to air raid shelters it would have been inconceivable for us bus them around to play football. We had similar responsibilities for the UK student volunteers and, desperate though I was to see the project go ahead, I could not countenance taking them into to a region that was rapidly deteriorating into a war zone. I borrowed Jane's mobile phone and called the party leaders at Stanstead and told them that the project was being postponed.

Any doubts that we had made the wrong decision were soon dissipated in the following days as the border skirmish developed into a full-fledged war between the IDF and Hezbollah, and missiles were raining down across the

Galilee hitting many of our project host communities such as Akko, Afula, Nazareth, and Tiberias. I managed to scramble onto a flight back to England later the next day and as I sat watching the coast of Israel fade into the distance I wondered if peace would ever come to this troubled land and, in the light of war breaking out yet again, what if anything the future might hold for Football for Peace.

I had another dilemma. Had the project gone ahead, I should have been flying directly from Tel Aviv to Durban in South Africa to present a paper at the International Sociological Associations World Congress. The paper was to have been based upon a critical reflection on the 2006 F4P experience. As I was committed to giving some kind of presentation I had to rethink my approach. Even though the 2006 project had to be postponed, there had been some valuable lessons learned and, as I sat in the clouds, I made the following notes which became the basis for my presentation in Durban:

1. Despite what legendary Liverpool FC Manager Bill Shankley may or may not have said, Football is not more important than life and death;
2. In a war zone self-preservation is the overriding motive for action both for the victims of conflict and for would-be peace-makers;
3. In a region experiencing serious internecine conflict, culturally focused peace initiatives can work only when preceded by military and political accommodations;
4. Culturally focused peace initiatives work best within maturing peace processes;
5. Complex political and social problems are usually unresponsive to simplistic solutions;
6. Approaching conflict resolution in a segmented and piecemeal fashion is unlikely to achieve sustainable results;
7. Adopting a stance of impartiality/neutrality is difficult to sustain when a context of injustice prevails and intensifies.

In addition to these observations I noted the following important questions:

1. Can conflict resolution and co-existence be promoted between Jewish and (Palestinian) Arab citizens within Israel while conflict between Israel and the Palestinian Authority and between Israel and neighbouring Arab countries rages?
2. Should we be engaging with sporting initiatives in the 'abnormal' society that constitutes the state of Israel?

3. Should we be developing partnerships with institutions of the Israeli State such as the Israeli Sports Authority and Ministry of Education?

4. How to respond to those who say that the central role played by the British Council in the project leads to the conclusion that Football for Peace is just another exercise in neo-imperialism?

5. Is mobilising a westernised, left-liberal agenda to encourage the equal participation of women in sport in countries with strong and conservative religious traditions merely another form of cultural imperialism?

As ever, we sociologists are usually much better at identifying social problems than we are at finding solutions and these are all very hard questions to which I have no easy answers. Faced with such imponderables and in the light of what happened in 2006 we could not be blamed for shelving F4P indefinitely as yet another — albeit small — failed peace initiative in the Middle East. Yet when I remember the disappointment etched deeply in the faces of our Jewish and Arab partners when they knew the project had to be cancelled, and think of the children and grown-ups who never had the opportunity to make new friends because we could not go and run our camps, I am minded otherwise. This does not mean that we should ignore the questions and issues highlighted above. Rather, they become part of the reflective and critical framework within which Football for Peace will continue to evolve. I am also reminded of the words of the eighteenth century political philosopher, Edmund Burke: that "the only thing necessary for the triumph of evil is for good men to do nothing". If invited, we'll be back to continue trying to do something.

INDEX